SWCA Anthropological Research Paper Number 10

Animas–La Plata Project:

Volume I — Cultural Resources Research and Sampling Design

James M. Potter

Phoenix_2006

Series Editors:
Michael S. Foster
Jean H. Ballagh

Technical Editor:
Cynthia Manseau

Principal Investigator:
James M. Potter

TABLE OF CONTENTS

List of Figures

List of Tables

Appendixes

Acknowledgments

This research design was written in November 2001 in response to a request for proposals by the Ute Mountain Ute Tribe, the contractor for the cultural resources work carried out as part of the Animas–La Plata Project. At the request of the Tribe, the research design has been revised for publication. Many individuals contributed to this document in various ways. Discussions with Jerry Fetterman helped place the project area and its associated cultural resources within a regional "big picture" context. Jerry also provided draft chapters of his Mid-America Pipeline Company report (Horn et al. 2003), which documents the most recent excavation work conducted in Ridges Basin and on Blue Mesa. Dr. Jim Allison offered ideas on the role ceramics could play in answering the questions being asked. Dr. Carl Phagan did the same for lithic artifacts, as did Dr. Karen Adams for botanical remains, Dr. Elizabeth Perry for human osteological data, and Dr. Kirk Anderson for geomorphological data. Dennis Gilpin supplied much of the information and many of the ideas in the Protohistoric and historic Euroamerican sections of the research design. Tom Yoder and Jason Chuipka deserve much of the credit for Appendix A, the ALP Field Manual. Finally, Tom Motsinger, at that time SWCA's Vice President for Cultural Resources, provided moral and administrative support for the labor that went into this research design. It was his enthusiasm from the outset that spurred us to carry out what has become a remarkable project and to produce this document.

Animas–La Plata Project:
Cultural Resources Research and Sampling Design

James M. Potter

INTRODUCTION

The Animas–La Plata reservoir project is in La Plata County, Colorado, just south of the modern town of Durango (Figure 1). Most of the archaeological sites that will be impacted by this project are in Ridges Basin, the site of the reservoir, and on Blue Mesa, a small prominence immediately east of Ridges Basin on the west bank of the Animas River (Figure 2). The reservoir will be formed by constructing a 217-foot-high earthen dam across a narrow canyon between the basin and the river and when full will cover approximately 1,500 acres in the Basin Creek drainage west of the river. The borrow area for dam fill will be on Blue Mesa. The Ute Mountain Ute Tribe, as contractor, retained SWCA

Environmental Consultants to undertake the required archaeological and cultural investigations in Ridges Basin and on Blue Mesa. This volume, the first of a projected 16 that will document the results of the ALP project (Appendix A), is SWCA's research design for the treatment of archaeological resources that will be impacted by the construction and filling of the reservoir. The volume includes a brief history of the archaeological work conducted, a discussion of the research questions that SWCA posed, and the field, laboratory, and analytical methods used to compile the information needed to address these questions. Though much of the work has been completed as this volume is published, much still remains to be done, and the description of the work here is in the form of the original proposal.

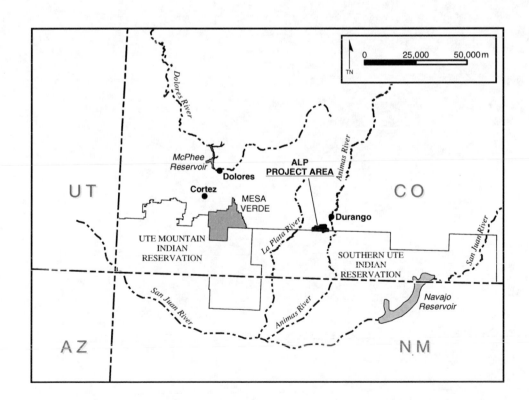

Figure 1. Location of ALP project area.

James M. Potter

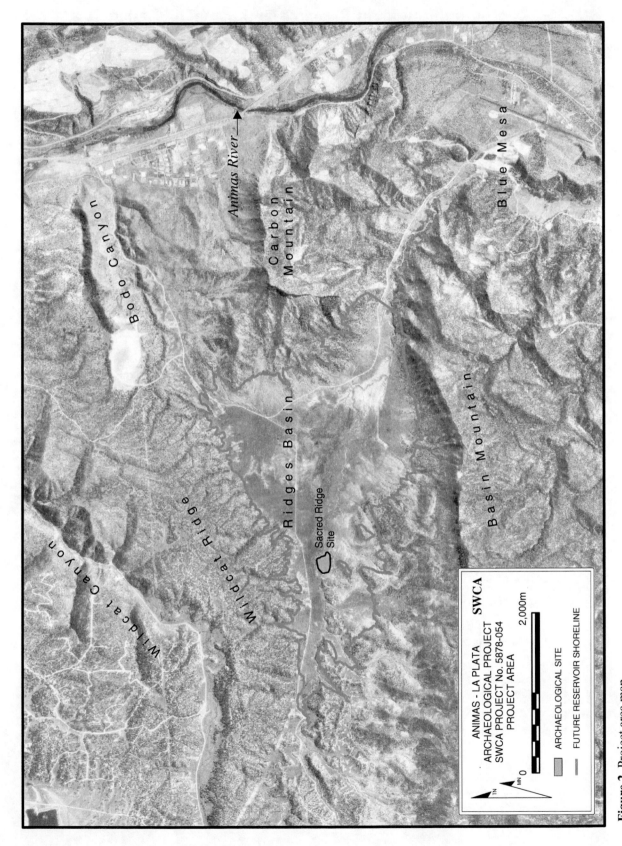

Figure 2. Project area map.

The Setting

Ridges Basin is a broad triangular basin bounded on the south by Basin Mountain, on the east by Carbon Mountain, and on the northwest by Wildcat Ridge. Basin Creek flows west to east through the basin, intersecting with the Animas River about one mile east of Ridges Basin. Bodo Canyon defines the northern extent of Ridges Basin between Carbon Mountain and Wildcat Ridge. When the ALP project is completed water will be pumped from the Animas River up Bodo Canyon into Ridges Basin, which will be dammed along Basin Creek at the intersection of Carbon Mountain and Basin Mountain.

The area is at about 6,800 feet in elevation and is rich in wild animals and plants, including elk, deer, wild turkey, raptors, piñon pine, ponderosa pine, and juniper. The soils in the basin are heavily laden with clay from the surrounding decomposing Lewis Shale formation. Blue Mesa, on the other hand, contains deep eolian soils, which would have been better for dryland farming.

The area is of interest to archaeologists for a number of reasons. First, there have been only sporadic episodes of systematic excavation conducted in the area, so in a lot of ways it represents a sizable hole in the prehistory of the Southwest. Thus, any data collected as part of the ALP project will be important to filling in that hole. Second, Durango contains some of the most interesting Basketmaker II sites in the Southwest, and more excavation in the area is bound to shed additional light on this extremely interesting and important time period. Third, examining the numerous early Pueblo I sites in the area will broaden our understanding of the earliest attempts at village aggregation in the Southwest and potentially address the issue of why the area was abandoned in the early 800s, never to be occupied again until Euroamericans settled there in the 1800s.

History of Archaeological Work in the Project Area

The 71 sites that SWCA proposes to investigate (Table 1; Figure 2) were identified, and in some cases excavated, in a series of formal and informal studies beginning in the early part of the twentieth century and in

Table 1. Proposed ALP Project Sites

Site No. (5LP)	Site No. (5LP)
169	498
171	503
174	508
175	510
176	511
177[1]	525
178	536
179[1]	537
181	545
182	549
183	567
184	569
185	570
186	577
187	578
188	579
192	588
235	601
236[2]	608
237[3]	614
238[4]	630[8]
239	634
240[5]	635
241[6]	1095
242[6]	2026
243[1]	2027
244	2029
245[7]	2086
246	2089
248	2091
452	2263
482	2264
484	2265
487	4870
495	6634
496	

Previous work:
[1]Pasture Ruin site? Root 1967/FLC
[2]Hoodoo Site/Root 1969/FLC
[3]Probably Root 1965/FLC
[4]Ives 1967/FLC
[5]Ives 1968, Duke 1981/FLC
[6]Ives 1968/FLC
[7]Sacred Ridge Site/Root 1966, 1967/FLC
[8]Duke 1981 FLC

earlier phases of the ALP project. Not all of the early work was reported or mapped, and the current site numbering system, devised by the Smithsonian Institution ("5" represents Colorado; "LP" represents La Plata County; the number following LP represents the consecutive numbering of sites in that county), was not used universally until the 1960s, so in a number of cases we cannot be certain just which sites were the subject of these studies. Sites discussed that are not included in the proposed work are in italics.

In the 1920s and 1930s, I. F. "Zeke" Flora, a local avocational archaeologist, excavated a number of ruins in the Durango area, including two unidentified sites in Ridges Basin and, with Harold Gladwin, an unknown number of sites on Blue Mesa. In his *History of the Ancient Southwest*, Gladwin (1957) briefly mentioned the Blue Mesa excavations and noted that in 1934 Gila Pueblo acquired more than 500 vessels from the Durango area, primarily from Blue Mesa. Gladwin supplied details of only one site, a subrectangular pit house more than 10 meters across with a 60-centimeter-wide bench around the entire circumference. The structure also contained adobe wingwalls and a tunnel ventilator shaft, and four large main-support post holes were in the floor.

According to Dean (1975), one of the Blue Mesa sites excavated by Flora (Ignacio 16:1) yielded a non-cutting date of A.D. 754. In addition, six pit house sites that Flora excavated on the Harper Ranch along the Upper Basin Creek drainage and two sites (Ignacio 11:1 and 11:4) on the saddle between Basin Creek and the Animas date within the seventh and eighth centuries (Dean 1975).

From 1965 to 1969 Fort Lewis College archaeological field schools excavated eleven sites in Ridges Basin and conducted surface collections at a number of other sites. In 1965, under the direction of Homer Root, the field school excavated an early Pueblo site containing a large pit structure, twelve jacal surface rooms, and a midden. Although Bonan's (1985) description of the Fort Lewis excavations suggested that this site may be 5LP171, and Ware (1986) contended that it is 5LP246, 5LP237 is more likely. All three sites have been disturbed by either previous excavation or pot hunting in surface room areas, but 5LP237 is the only one with a previously

excavated pit house, and its location is consistent with Root's description.

Bonan (1985) also reported that Root's 1966 field school excavated three sites on a ridge at the southern edge of Ridges Basin, identified as 5LP245, 5LP256, and 5LP604. However, the work in fact occurred entirely at 5LP245, now referred to as the "Sacred Ridge Site," a large village with more than ten aggregated pit structures. Root excavated three pit structures, two shallow circular structures (described as "dance areas"), 28 surface rooms, and more than 40 burials in various middens at the site. According to Bonan, two habitations were completely excavated and five others were tested. No formal report exists on these excavations, but the excavators took photographs, including aerial photos, and some of Root's notes survive.

Root conducted excavations at four sites in 1967, Pasture Ruins I, II, and III on an alluvial fan at the east end of Ridges Basin and North Ruin I northeast of Ridges Basin in what is now Bodo Industrial Park (Ware 1986:87). Bonan (1985) suggested that the Pasture Ruins sites are 5LP177, 5LP179, and 5LP243. The site records describe these sites as jacal habitation units, but the field school excavated only surface rooms and midden units. The field school removed three burials from the midden at Pasture Ruin I. Root also conducted further excavations at 5LP245 (the Sacred Ridge Site) in 1967, but he made no record of the exact location or the extent of this work (Root 1967).

Dr. John "Doc" Ives also conducted a Fort Lewis College field school in Ridges Basin in 1967, at 5LP238, a large habitation unit near the Bodo ranch house (5LP579). The site consisted of a jacal-adobe room block and a front-oriented pit house, which apparently contained a number of disarticulated human skeletal remains. No further details of the pit house or rooms have been reported, although a detailed site map from the excavation exists.

In 1968 Ives targeted surface rooms at three sites on the same alluvial fan as Homer Root's "Pasture" sites. According to Ware (1986:88), these sites were 5LP240, 5LP241, and 5LP242, which Ives interpreted as field houses. Subsequent work (conducted by SWCA in 2003 as part of the ALP project) indicates that these sites are habitation units with pit houses. No reports of Ives's excavations were completed.

In 1969 Root returned to Ridges Basin for a final season, focusing on a single site on the northern slopes of Ridges Basin. Site 5LP236, the "Hoodoo Site," consisted of a jacal room block, a pit house, and scattered trash southeast of the pit house. Root briefly described the room block in his notes as ten contiguous jacal rooms, each measuring 3.5 by 3 m, all plastered and well constructed. However, no detailed descriptions or drawings of the room block architecture appear to have been made. Root did mention that a quantity of ground stone was recovered from the structure. Root described the pit house, excavated by backhoe, as a circular structure over 8 m in diameter and 2.4 m deep containing a bench, seven main-support post holes, a double-holed vent shaft, and plastered wingwalls. A sand-filled "heating pit" was noted in the floor, but no formal hearth. Finally, burned human remains were recovered from the floor of the pit house. A "field observation" by Zeke Flora of a tree-ring sample yielded a construction date of A.D. 712 for the pit structure, but this date cannot be substantiated.

None of the excavations directed by Root and Ives between 1965 and 1969 were thoroughly documented. It is clear, though, based on subsequent work in the area, that all of the sites they excavated belonged to the early Pueblo I period (A.D. 700–850) and consistently comprised a pit house with associated jacal rooms and a trash area. The number, orientation, and arrangement of these elements were variable, however. In 1974 and 1975, under the direction of Ives, the Fort Lewis College field school excavated two identified early Pueblo I sites on Blue Mesa. The results have not been published.

In 1975 two large-scale surveys were conducted in the project area, one on Blue Mesa and one in Ridges Basin. Ives and Barry Hibbets of Fort Lewis College directed the Blue Mesa survey, in the same area surveyed by Gladwin and Flora in 1935 (Ware 1986:90), and recorded 46 early Pueblo I sites with pit house depressions. The survey of Ridges Basin, conducted by the University of Colorado, was an intensive inventory of the eastern portion of the basin below the 6,960-foot elevation line (Leidy 1976) that recorded and surface-collected 37 sites. This survey was the first in a history of rampant surface collection of sites in Ridges Basin as part of archaeological surveys.

In 1979 and 1980 Woods Canyon Archaeological Consultants recorded eight sites within the segment of the Mid-America Pipeline Company corridor extending through Ridges Basin and over Blue Mesa (Fetterman and Honeycutt 1982) and excavated two sites on the mesa, *5LP378* and *5LP379*. Site 5LP378 contained three burned surface room blocks and one probable pit structure. Excavation of one of the surface room blocks revealed that it consisted of three contiguous rooms and possibly two more. A tree-ring sample from the site yielded a date of A.D. 782. Site 5LP379 contained a surface room block, a pit structure, and a shallow midden, all of which were excavated. Tree-ring dates from the site place the occupation between A.D. 831 and 839, the latest occupation recorded in the Durango area.

In 1980 and 1981 ESCA-Tech Corporation and their subcontractor, the University of New Mexico's Office of Contract Archeology (Winter et al. 1986), conducted an intensive Class III survey of Ridges Basin. This survey identified 196 sites. Of these, 105 contained Pueblo I ceramics, 12 had late Pueblo I–Pueblo III ceramics, 25 produced Basketmaker II or earlier projectile points, and 36 were Euroamerican sites (Winter et al. 1986:231). The work included magnetometer investigations at 30 of the Pueblo I and possible Basketmaker sites (Bennett and Weymouth 1986). Several important results emerged from this survey. The first was the systematic identification and recording of all site types in Ridges Basin. Previous archaeological work had tended to focus exclusively on large habitation sites with surface room blocks, pit houses, and refuse deposits, that is, sites with a high likelihood of yielding whole pots, datable charcoal, and tree-ring samples. The ESCA-Tech survey provided some of the first data on prehistoric sites and activities outside the range of primary habitation. As John Ware has suggested,

> Most of the early research in the Durango area was conducted by amateur archaeologists whose primary interest lay in amassing large, personal collections of artifacts, and by professional archaeologists interested in documenting early Basketmaker culture in the northern San Juan Basin and extending the tree-ring chronol-

ogy back to the early centuries of the Christian era. Given these two overriding objectives, it is not surprising that a bias developed in the selection of sites for excavation and strategies of data recovery [Ware 1986:92].

Pueblo I sites documented by the ESCA-Tech/OCA survey were of two main types: (1) habitation sites with surface rooms, at least one pit structure, and midden deposits; and (2) limited-activity sites lacking architecture. A second result of the survey was the identification of a bimodal size distribution for aceramic lithic scatters. As a result, Archaic period sites became a significant aspect of the archaeological record and research potential of Ridges Basin.

In 1981 and 1982 Fort Lewis College conducted another field school in Ridges Basin. In 1981 Phil Duke directed excavation of Site 5LP630, near Root's "Pasture Sites." The site contained an unburned early Pueblo I pit structure, a burned surface room block, and a shallow midden. Scattered human remains were recovered from the pit house. In addition, the field school tested 5LP240 (referred to as 5LP242 in Duke's report), a site that had been excavated by Ives, but uncovered no additional features (Duke 1985).

In 1982, under the direction of Duke and Susan Riches, the Fort Lewis College field school tested three limited-activity sites, *5LP491*, *5LP493*, and *5LP593*. The only subsurface features discovered were three slab-lined cists at 5LP593 (Duke 1985).

In the 1980s Complete Archaeological Services Associates (CASA) conducted various work in the ALP project area. CASA relocated, re-recorded, and once again surface-collected the 196 sites recorded by ESCA-Tech/OCA, updated all of the site cards. They also systematically surveyed the Wheeler and Koshak Borrow Areas east of Ridges Basin, recording 46 sites in the Wheeler Borrow Area on Blue Mesa and three in the Koshak Borrow Area (Fuller 1988a).

CASA also conducted excavations at 11 sites in Bodo Canyon, adjacent to the north edge of Ridges Basin, as part of the Uranium Mill Tailings Remedial Action Project, or UMTRA (Fuller 1988b). The Bodo Canyon excavations treated two late Archaic hunting camps,

four early Pueblo I habitations, and five early Pueblo I nonhabitation sites (three artifact scatters and two possible field house sites). In addition, two of the Bodo Canyon sites (*5LP478A* and *5LP1104*) contained Basketmaker II components, both with shallow, basin-shaped pit houses, hearths, storage pits, and midden deposits. Radiocarbon date ranges for the Basketmaker II components were A.D. 180±70 to 440±60 at 5LP478A, and A.D. 270±80 to 280±80 at 5LP1104. Fuller (1988b) proposed that these sites represented permanent habitations. However, seasonal occupation during the winter months may be more consistent with the quantity and diversity of artifacts recovered from these sites and with models of Basketmaker II settlement in the San Juan Basin (e.g., Hogan 1985; Hogan et al. 1991). Fuller's work constitutes the first and, to date, only data on Basketmaker II sites in the project area, highlighting the potential of this area to yield significant data on sites dating to this time period.

In 1990 the Bureau of Reclamation synthesized survey and excavation work undertaken to that time and had the project area designated an archaeological district eligible for the National Register of Historic Places. In 1992 and 1993 Northern Arizona University (NAU) and their subcontractor, La Plata Archaeological Consultants, mapped and surface-collected 42 archaeological sites in Ridges Basin. NAU and the Bureau of Reclamation published seven volumes on the results of this limited work (Allison 1995; Gregg and Smiley 1995; Gregg, Smiley, and Folb 1995; Smiley 1995; Smiley and Folb 1997; Smiley and Gregg 1995; Smiley and Robins 1997), further documenting the variation represented by the artifact assemblages in Ridges Basin.

Finally, in the late 1990s Woods Canyon Archaeological Consultants excavated three sites—*5LP203*, *5LP379*, and *5LP515*—in or near the ALP project area as part of the Mid-America Pipeline Project (Horn et al. 2003). Site 5LP203, on the southeastern slope of Blue Mesa just above the Animas, contained a single pit structure, a room block remnant, a cobble apron, a trash midden, a roasting pit, and a low-density artifact scatter. Site 5LP379, on Blue Mesa, contained two pit structures (one of which yielded the late tree-ring date reported by Woods Canyon in the early 1980s), a poorly preserved room block remnant, and a midden. Site 5LP515, in Ridges Basin near the proposed dam site at the eastern end of the basin, consisted of a pit house, a room block with two surface structures and three extramural features, and a trash midden. Each of these sites dates to the early Pueblo I period.

All of this earlier work has set the stage for the current research design, which is by no means the first to be written for the project area. As far back as 1978, Nickens (1978) wrote a cultural resources evaluation for the Animas–La Plata project that identified and outlined the research significance of the area. Since that time a number of research designs for data recovery have been proposed (e.g., Fuller 1989; Smiley and Gregg 1995), leading up to the current incarnation of the project. This document owes much to these efforts. However, as will be readily apparent, our theoretical orientation differs significantly from these earlier research programs, which tended to be more ecological and "adaptationist" in focus. It is our theoretical perspective, looking at the interplay among human adaptations to changing environmental conditions, the role of human agency, and the historical contingency of evolutionary change, that sets the current research design apart from earlier proposals.

PREHISTORIC RESEARCH DESIGN

The ALP project sites will provide substantial information on three of the most significant archaeological issues worldwide: (1) the hunting and gathering lifeway, (2) the origins of food production, and (3) the transition to settled village life. Archaic period sites documented in the project area will add to our understanding of hunter-gatherers; Early Formative (Late Archaic/Basketmaker II) sites will contribute to understanding the transition to agriculture in the Southwest; and the numerous Pueblo I period sites in the project area will add to our knowledge of the origins of settled village life. The particular manifestation of each of these developments in the project area will both add incrementally to broader cultural evolutionary patterns and deepen our understanding of variation in the historical trajectories of groups in the Four Corners region.

SWCA's theoretical approach to the ALP project stresses the comparable importance of human adaptations to changing environmental conditions, the role of human agency, and the historical contingency of evolutionary change. This tripartite perspective recognizes

that the organization of actors and groups within a region, their perception of the landscape, the decisions they make at the household and community levels, and the actions they ultimately take are largely structured by both the immediate environmental and social conditions in which they live and what has come before, that is, their history. Thus, although environmental and social conditions affect or constrain the behaviors and influence the ideologies of a given group, that group's history, its place of origin, its established connections to places and other groups, and the ways it has coped in the past with environmental, population, and resource stresses, all directly affect its response to these stimuli at any given point. In addition, human agency—the choices people make as they take action to realize their goals—plays a role in their responses. In other words, individuals are not just passive receptacles of culture and "norms," they are conscious actors or agents with diverse aims who draw upon and manipulate resources to their strategic advantage. Yet these actors are socially constituted beings who are embedded in socio-cultural structures and ecological surroundings that both define their goals and constrain their actions. In this view, cultural patterning is viewed as a long-term process resulting from the interplay of historically constituted structure(s), human agency, and environmental adaptations, rather than simply as an adaptive response to particular environmental stimuli.

The ALP project has two unique aspects. The first is its areal extent and the fact that it encompasses two adjacent, densely occupied, roughly contemporaneous locales—Ridges Basin and Blue Mesa. This circumstance will allow not only a comparison of the two areas, but also an intensive study of broad settlement patterns through excavation that is rarely possible anymore. The second is the short but intensive occupation during the early Pueblo I period (A.D. 750-825), ending an apparent 400-year occupational hiatus following the Basketmaker II period. The Puebloan occupation is not an example of long-term adaptation to a specific set of local environmental conditions. Groups migrated into Ridges Basin, potentially from different areas of the Southwest, at about A.D. 750 and organized themselves into one or more large, dispersed communities that apparently lasted only a generation or two. A primary focus of the prehistoric research design is to understand how these early Puebloan groups came together and organized themselves on the landscape, and why in a fairly short time they left, never to return. While environmental variables undoubtedly were factors in these processes, we are also interested in the social and historical factors that were at play.

What is particularly intriguing about the groups that settled in Ridges Basin in the eighth century is that they may have had different cultural origins, and thus brought with them different histories. If so, how much of this historical/cultural differentiation persisted in the face of village aggregation is an important empirical question that this research will address. It may have been the case, for instance, that a new system of integration was developed that de-emphasized particular group histories, or it could be that particular histories were emphasized over others. How group differences were incorporated (either actively or passively) into the organizational structure of the Ridges Basin system is the crux of the Pueblo I research proposed here.

In addition, SWCA proposes to develop behavioral and social models that will allow comparisons of the historical and cultural make-up of groups in the ALP area with those occupying other sub-regions. Our main premise is that differences noted between the Ridges Basin and Blue Mesa groups and contemporary groups residing (for example) to the west of the La Plata River are as much about historical and cultural (and perhaps linguistic) variation as they are about resource distributions and other environmental differences. This perspective requires a broad comparative view of patterning in the region, as well as a finely detailed "close-up" view of material patterning within the Ridges Basin area. Thus, various scales of analysis, ranging from the individual activity area or household to the sub-region or region, will be used to construct the historical trajectory of Ridges Basin area inhabitants.

Given this theoretical perspective and the nature of the archaeological record of the project area, the prehistoric research is organized into three problem domains: (1) the hunting and gathering lifeway in southwestern Colorado, (2) the transition to agriculture in this region, and (3) early Puebloan occupation in the Ridges Basin area. The research design presented here draws heavily from previous research designs for the ALP project as well as the recent Context Volume for the Southern Colorado

River Basin (Lipe et al. 1999). Specific research issues to be addressed are (1) site structure and settlement, (2) subsistence, (3) local and regional population growth and abandonment, (4) mobility-sedentism and land use, and (5) historical patterns of social and economic organization. Methodologically, refining chronology, environmental context, inter- and intrasite comparisons, and regional and intra-regional comparisons will be emphasized throughout.

Problem Domain 1: The Hunting and Gathering Lifeway

For this project, the Archaic period is defined as extending from about 7500 B.C. to the local introduction of maize circa 1000–500 B.C. (Lipe and Pitblado 1999:106). In other words, we equate "Archaic" with a post-Paleoindian, pre-agricultural hunting and gathering lifeway.

The Archaic record of Southwestern Colorado is much sparser and less well understood than that of adjacent regions. One explanation for this local paucity of evidence of Archaic occupation and use is that Archaic groups tended to exploit lower sandy grassland areas more intensively than upland piñon-juniper environments. It is also possible that much of the Archaic occupation of the area is masked by the heavy Ancestral Puebloan occupation in the Four Corners region. Nevertheless, there is good evidence of Late Archaic occupation in and around Ridges Basin, as well as ephemeral Early and Middle Archaic use of the area (Fuller 1988b; Smiley 1995).

SWCA's goals are to reconstruct the subsistence strategy, social organization, settlement pattern, and sociocultural ties of local Archaic hunters and gatherers. We will do this by (1) collecting direct and indirect evidence on site function and subsistence; (2) establishing classifications of site types and examining what they tell us about Archaic subsistence strategies, social organization, and settlement patterns; and (3) investigating the geographic distribution of lithic materials to collect data about mobility, exchange networks, and regional interaction during the Archaic period. Finally, we wish to ascertain the date and process by which people in the project area adopted agriculture.

Research Issue 1.1: Archaic Site Structure and Settlement

Ware (1986) has defined two basic Archaic site types for Ridges Basin: large and small lithic artifact scatters. The large sites are extensive scatters of flaked stone debris, ground stone items, and projectile points; these sites may have features and tend to occur in the west end of Ridges Basin. They have been interpreted in two ways. Ware (1981) views them as loci that were used repeatedly for hundreds of years as seasonal hunting camps for procuring deer and elk during their seasonal migrations through the Wildcat Canyon area. Fuller (1988b:340), on the other hand, suggested that large Archaic lithic artifact scatters may represent winter base camps, which should be near water, fuel, shelter, game, and concentrations of piñon trees, all of which occur in the west end of Ridges Basin.

Detailed site function studies are needed to test these two alternative hypotheses. If Ware's hunting camp hypothesis is correct, we would expect (1) remains from manufacturing and repair of hunting tool kits (including a large proportion of projectile points), (2) uniformity of flaked stone assemblage characteristics across each site (reflecting their narrow focus), (3) a similarly narrow range of species and bone elements in faunal assemblages, and (4) placement on the landscape to maximize access to large game. If Fuller's base camp hypothesis is true, we would expect (1) diverse artifact assemblages, (2) multiple features (possibly including storage features to hold food for the lean months), (3) ground stone, (4) a diverse faunal assemblage, and (5) positioning on the landscape to maximize access to a variety of resources. Initial data tend to support the winter base camp hypothesis, but these data are scanty, and the two hypotheses require further testing. Also, multiple site types may be represented in the Ridges Basin sample, and functional variation may be much more complex than the two models suggest. Documenting the full range of functional variation in large Archaic lithic artifact scatters (and how that variation might change) is therefore of primary concern.

These models do not account for the small lithic artifact scatters, which are widely distributed within Ridges Basin. Fuller (1988b) indicated that variation among some of these smaller sites reflects functional differences: some are hunting camps, whereas others are plant procurement sites. He also noted, however, that differentiating the two site types based on surface characteristics is difficult, and that the small lithic artifact scatters are likely to represent other site types as well. Moreover, if large lithic scatters represent seasonal base camps, a particular set of small lithic scatters may represent satellite procurement sites (Binford's [1980] collector model). On the other hand, if larger lithic artifact sites are palimpsests of repeated use for a particular task, such as hunting, smaller sites may not be functionally linked with them at all. (Indeed, they may be locales of just one or two instances of the same activity carried out at the larger sites.)

Interestingly, Billman (1997) has found that Archaic land use strategies on the Ute Mountain piedmont to the west of ALP changed over time. Middle Archaic sites in the area fit the expectations of satellite sites of a collector-based settlement system: small, limited-activity sites with no structures or features, occupied by small groups for brief episodes. Corresponding base camps are thought to have been in upland piñon-juniper environments. During the Late Archaic this episodic land-use strategy shifted to one of single-household residential camps occupied during the spring, when people harvested seed-bearing grasses, hunted deer and antelope, and stored food in well-made pit structures.

Documenting in detail the functional and chronological variation in Archaic period sites in the ALP project area should enable us to reconstruct these larger land-use patterns through time. In addition, a Geographic Information System (GIS) study of the distribution of ALP Archaic site types relative to plant communities, water, other resources, and other, contemporaneous sites would be a useful way to address which variables are structuring the location of site types on the landscape and what particular land use model (e.g., a "vegetative diversity model" versus a "serial-forager model" [Fuller 1988b], or some other model that considers social as well as ecological variables) best accounts for the observed variation. Therefore, SWCA will implement a GIS analysis of Ridges Basin settlement, drawing on the new site-function data obtained through excavation.

Archaeologists working on the Four Corners Archaic occupation (Hogan 1986; Reher 1977; Vierra 1985;

Vogler 1982) have carried on a long-standing debate about whether functional site types can be identified or whether differences in artifact assemblages resulted from other variables, such as the size of the group that occupied a site, the duration of occupation, or the number of times a site was used. This issue has important implications for the proposed studies of Archaic period subsistence, social organization, and settlement. Project area sites with preserved fire pits may help resolve this issue. The degree of formality of fire pits (e.g., whether lined with rock or clay) suggests whether the use was intended to be short term or long term. By directly dating each fire pit, analyzing its contents for pollen, macrobotanical plant remains, and faunal remains, analyzing the associated artifacts, and recording its spatial relationship to other fire pits, SWCA will be able to determine the plants and animals being processed, the number of social groups represented, the duration of occupation, and the number of occupants. Variation in artifact assemblages that cannot be explained by these factors can then be attributed to more stochastic processes such as artifact discard. The resulting improved understanding of the structure and function of Archaic period components with associated fire pits can then be applied to interpreting Archaic sites in general, including sites where fire pits are not found.

Although Southwest archaeologists are notoriously lax about stratigraphy in open-air sites, we should attempt to define stratigraphic relationships in the large Archaic lithic artifact scatters, particularly if features are present. If a site was used sporadically over many centuries, fire pits and other features might have been built at different levels as the site surface slowly aggraded or deflated. In contrast, if a site was used intensively over short periods, all of the fire pits and other features should originate from a single ground surface.

For all this to work, it is necessary to find and expose an adequate sample of features in their stratigraphic contexts. The now-traditional discovery method of mechanical grading and stripping is good for exposing large numbers of features, but at the price of destroying the associated use surfaces and removing the artifacts on those surfaces. In particular, mechanical exposure identifies pit features by scraping below their rims, destroying the stratigraphic tie-in between the pit and the surface from which it was created. For the ALP project,

SWCA therefore proposes to conduct magnetometer and soil resistivity studies at Archaic (and Basketmaker II) sites to locate possible subsurface features within sites, then hand-expose defined features so that they remain in association with their use surfaces and the artifacts on those surfaces. We will phase this experimental research, beginning with a pilot study on one or more sites with a potential for subsurface features to explore which technique or combination of techniques works best to locate hearths and other pit features. If this approach is successful, a larger sample of sites will be investigated using the refined techniques.

Research Issue 1.2: Archaic Subsistence

While archaeologists have known for several decades that Archaic period groups ate a variety of wild plant and animal foods, the exact make-up of this diet and the timing of various dietary mixes has yet to be resolved. This is especially the case when cultigens are added to the subsistence system. Previous research on this topic has shown that Archaic period groups made use of a variety of wild plant foods; the chenopodium and amaranth families were especially important in Archaic subsistence. Maize was apparently introduced in the Middle Archaic, perhaps as early as 3800 B.P., and became more widespread during the Late Archaic. Squash was part of the Archaic diet by at least 3000 B.P., although its cultivation or use was apparently even more limited than that of maize. What is clear is that date of arrival of domesticates is far earlier than the date of commitment to maize agriculture, which is still debated (Huckell 1995; Matson 1991; Wills 1996). Therefore, in examining Archaic period remains, SWCA will focus heavily on quantifying changes in subsistence during the Archaic.

Three primary issues regarding Archaic subsistence will be examined in the ALP project area—subsistence mix through time, the timing of the introduction of maize agriculture into the diet, and the conditions under which hunter-gatherers incorporated agriculture into their subsistence system. Addressing the first and second issues depends heavily on chronometric control. Conventional radiocarbon and accelerator mass spectrometry (AMS) dating of annuals, in conjunction with obsidian hydration and relative dating techniques, will be conducted on as many samples as necessary (or possible). Reconstructing subsistence mix through time can be approached through the identification and quantification of floral and faunal remains, analysis of catchment areas, analysis of assemblage characteristics, analysis of processing or other facilities, use wear studies, and analysis of residue on tools. Dating the earliest maize in the project area will require radiocarbon dating of maize samples recovered from Archaic hearths or other pit features. Small samples of maize remains may be dated using AMS methods. Finally, understanding the conditions under which maize was introduced into the subsistence mix requires consideration of regional population levels, settlement organization, environmental conditions, the status of hunted and gathered resources, mobility options, changes in technology (including storage technology), and the nature and direction of non-local relations.

Research Issue 1.3: Mobility and Interregional Relationships

During the Archaic period, residential mobility played a significant role in the use of lithic resources. Unlike the settled Ancestral Puebloans, who generally relied on local materials, Archaic period groups used a mix of local and non-local resources. They also made a variety of different projectile point styles, depending on their cultural affiliation. Thus, identifying lithic assemblage characteristics, lithic sourcing studies, and stylistic analyses of projectile points can help define patterns of mobility, territoriality, and interregional interaction during the Archaic period.

Lithic Assemblage Characteristics

Basic morphofunctional analysis of Archaic lithic assemblages will be an important part of identifying site function, including the possible range of resources exploited at or from a given site. Beyond this, however, we will focus on various attributes of Archaic lithic assemblages.

Technological Evidence on Sources and Patterns of Tool Stone Procurement

Most of the local tool stone in the Ridges Basin probably originated as cobbles collected in or near the basin. We expect that local origin to be obvious in the assemblages, and that the local stone will have been used more expediently because of its greater availability. For example, flakes of local stone may have a high proportion of surface cortex derived from the exterior of the source cobbles. Non-local stone (Smiley 1995; Warren 1986) probably entered the archaeological record by several means (including direct quarrying, collection from secondary sources such as cobble deposits, and exchange). Analysis of artifacts made from these materials can indicate whether the artifacts were created from prepared cores acquired in forays or were finished tools acquired through exchange, and thus will shed light on patterns of mobility and exchange.

Raw Material Diversity

Raw material diversity indices are another important source of information on tool stone acquisition and use. The number of raw material sources represented in an archaeological setting, along with the physical characteristics and relative abundance of each material, is a highly interpretable dataset quite independent of the locations of the sources, their precise petrographic/chemical signatures, and their distances from the archaeological context. Diversity measures on recognizable material groupings can be used as a proxy for the number of raw material sources for a given archaeological assemblage. We can therefore expand our analysis beyond the usual question—"Where did these items come from?"—to ask, "How many raw material sources contributed to this assemblage, and in what proportions?"

Lithic Sourcing Studies

In the Historic period, some hunter-gatherer bands (such as the Paiute) ranged over thousands of square kilometers. Is it possible to reconstruct the territory used by Archaic period hunter-gatherers? The distribution of flaked stone raw materials at Archaic sites in three basins in the Four Corners area suggests a possible methodology (Gilpin et al. 1999). San Juan Basin Archaic sites typically have artifacts of obsidian and Cerro Pedernal chert from the Jemez Mountains, Zuni Mountain chert, Washington Pass chert from Narbona Pass in the Chuska Mountains, and Brushy Basin chert from the Carrizo Mountains. Archaic sites in the Blanding Basin have stone artifacts made from Brushy Basin chert but never have artifacts of obsidian, Cerro Pedernal chert, Zuni Mountain chert, or Washington Pass chert. Archaic sites in the Chinle Valley typically have stone artifacts of white baked siltstone from Black Mesa, Brushy Basin chert from the Carrizo Mountains, Owl Rock chert from the Lukachukais, and Petrified Forest silicified wood from Beautiful Valley, but no artifacts of obsidian, Cerro Pedernal chert, Zuni Mountain chert, or Washington Pass chert. These patterns suggest an absence of trade between the basins.

In addition, frequencies of various lithic sources across the landscape suggest that during the Archaic period multiple groups were present within these basins and that each material type was traded independently in down-the-line exchange. This model can be further refined by collecting data on the distributions of lithic raw materials in additional areas, such as the Ridges Basin area, by examining the distributions during different time periods within the Archaic, and by investigating patterns of lithic raw material use and artifact discard. To explore these issues, SWCA will source and quantify lithic raw materials at Archaic sites, compare them with frequencies from other basins, and examine whether certain lithic raw materials were used for specific types of artifacts and how lithic raw material use might affect artifact discard.

Unlike in Ridges Basin, Archaic lithic assemblages recovered from the Ute Mountain Ute Irrigated Lands Archaeological Project were composed exclusively of materials found around Ute Mountain (Billman 1997). Ute Mountain Archaic groups probably had considerably smaller ranges than most Southwestern Archaic groups, including those in Ridges Basin. The investigators attributed the Ute Mountain pattern to that area's environmental diversity. SWCA will use the results of lithic source studies from the ALP project to conduct a GIS analysis comparing the territorial ranges of Ridges Basin Archaic groups with groups in the Ute Mountain area and analyze those patterns in terms of the environmental diversity available to the groups in each area at given points in time. The results of this analysis will help us evaluate the argument that environmental diversity was a factor in structuring annual ranges, and will shed light on how social territories were defined and maintained.

Projectile Point Stylistic Analyses

One of the more interesting patterns of the Archaic period is the development of regional historical traditions. Previous discussions of the Archaic in Southwestern Colorado have been based largely on Irwin-Williams's (1973, 1979) proposed Oshara tradition and phase sequence for the San Juan Basin (see, for example, Eddy et al. 1984). Irwin-Williams argued that the Oshara tradition extended across much of the Colorado Plateau during the Archaic and that the Ancestral Puebloan tradition developed in place from this earlier pattern. It is becoming clear, however, that Southwestern Colorado was home to a variety of groups and exhibited a complex array of socio-cultural ties during the Archaic period.

Smiley (1995) reported on Archaic period projectile points associated with aceramic sites in Ridges Basin. Most of the Middle Archaic points tended to resemble the "high" side-notched Sudden types of the northern Colorado Plateau rather than the points associated with the Middle Archaic in the Oshara sequence—suggesting at least some affiliation with northern groups during this period. SWCA is particularly interested in understanding where the Ridges Basin area groups fit with respect to the regional traditions that were developing at this time. Documenting mobility, range, and exchange patterns for Archaic groups and refining projectile point typologies should shed light on cultural affiliations and inter-areal relationships. These patterns are important because they set the stage for future interactions and developments and, ultimately, the historical trajectory for occupation of the Ridges Basin area by agricultural groups.

Problem Domain 2: The Transition to Agriculture

For this project, and consistent with the original Pecos classification, we define the Basketmaker II (BMII) period as the time span between the introduction of maize and the introduction of pottery, between 1000 B.C. and A.D. 500 (Lipe 1999:132). Because of the absence of pottery, BMII sites often are difficult to distinguish from Archaic period lithic sites; however, the overall pattern of BMII in the Ridges Basin area is quite distinctive (Morris and Burgh 1954:75–78). Diagnostic remains include corner-notched, expanding-stem dart points, T-shaped drills, trough and oval basin metates, a mix of one-hand and two-hand cobble mános, shallow, circular pit houses, and a variety of large storage pits. Matson (1991:45–46) also noted that basketry from Durango area BMII sites has a "half-rod-bundle foundation, with interlocking stitches." This design differs substantially from BMII basketry found to the west, which has a pattern of "two-rod-bundle foundation with non-interlocking stitches."

The distinctive character of the Durango area BMII sites and their material culture compared to the classic western BMII of the Cedar Mesa area has led Matson (1991) to suggest that they represent two related but different cultural traditions. This raises the question of the origins of BMII groups in the Durango area: do they have a fundamentally different history than BMII groups to the west? Matson (1991) suggested that the Durango BMII manifestation had cultural origins in indigenous Late Archaic groups, while BMII groups farther west may have descended culturally from migrants from the Sonoran Desert. Investigating the cultural origins of BMII groups in the Ridges Basin area is therefore an important research goal.

Additional goals include reconstructing the subsistence strategy, social organization, settlement pattern, and socio-cultural ties of BMII farmers in the project area. We propose to do this by (1) collecting direct and indirect evidence on site function and subsistence, (2) establishing classifications of site types and examining what they tell us about BMII subsistence strategies, social organization, and settlement patterns, and (3) investigating the geographic distribution of lithic materials to find out what can be learned about mobility, exchange networks, and regional interaction during the BMII period. Finally, we want to ascertain the date and process by which BMII people abandoned the project area and where they may have gone when they left.

Research Issue 2.1: Basketmaker II Site Structure and Settlement

Based on work on Cedar Mesa, Matson et al. (1988; Matson 1991:73–101) have recognized three basic site types for the BMII period: habitations, campsites, and limited-activity sites. Currently, BMII habitation sites in the Ridges Basin area are defined by (1) an absence of

ceramics, (2) a high frequency of cracked igneous cobbles, (3) burned adobe from structures, (4) BMII–style projectile points, and (5) magnetometer data indicating the possible presence of structures (Fuller 1988b:351). There appears to be considerable size variation in these sites, perhaps related to social differences, temporal differences (e.g., greater aggregation through time), or variable reuse of specific locations. Moreover, no current models exist that allow interpretation of BMII non-habitation sites in the Durango area.

Talus Village, a classic Durango area BMII site, has house units that exhibit evidence of repeated reoccupation, indicating movement in and out of the same site over a long period. While seasonal movement is a possibility, given the site's location near both river bottomland and upland wild resources, longer-term residence seems more likely.

Two sites (5LP478A and 5LP1104) excavated as part of the Uranium Mill Tailings Remedial Action Project (UMTRA) in Bodo Canyon, just north of Ridges Basin, contained BMII components. Both had shallow basin-shaped pit houses, hearths, storage pits, and midden deposits. Fuller (1988b) proposed that these sites may represent permanent habitations. However, seasonal occupation during the winter months may be more consistent with the quantity and diversity of the artifacts recovered from these sites and with models of BMII settlement in the San Juan Basin (e.g., Hogan 1985; Hogan et al. 1991). Additional data on BMII sites from the ALP project area should shed light on the debate and help to understand the variation of BMII sites in the region.

In attacking these problems, the basic approach will closely resemble that used for Archaic sites. Identifying and dating within BMII sites individual hearth areas, structures, activity areas, and functional site types will allow investigators to estimate site occupation spans, structure use-lives, and site populations, providing a dataset from which to build estimates of local population sizes and models of settlement and social organization. Documenting the variety and distribution of BMII sites in the Ridges Basin area is likely to be useful in delineating BMII settlement systems, a major concern of SWCA researchers. Settlement "clusters" are evident during the BMII period, one of them on the divide between Ridges Basin and Bodo Canyon (Fuller 1988b). At this time, however, it is not known whether such clusters contain contemporaneous structures or if particular settlements were reoccupied over time. Resolving this issue requires data on the use-lives of structures and the duration of occupation of individual sites (Varien and Potter 1997).

Improved chronologies are key in establishing feature contemporaneity and understanding settlement patterns through time. Matson (1991) has argued that the earliest BMII settlements should be associated with floodplain farming, but that by the late BMII period (A.D. 1–500), varieties of maize had been developed that permitted upland dry farming as well. Many late BMII sites in the Durango area appear to be oriented to floodplain settings in valleys with perennial streams. The exception to this pattern may be Ridges Basin, which has BMII sites in an upland farming area with good southern and eastern exposures. The date of these sites is in question, however. Dating BMII and "Late Archaic" components in the project area is essential for determining whether early BMII sites exist in the study area, and if they do, whether their distribution counters or supports Matson's hypothesis. Refined chronological controls would also allow for the construction of better models of BMII settlement and community patterns. Excavation of BMII pit structures has the potential to yield tree-ring and radiocarbon dates, which could be used to extend the Four Corners area tree-ring chronology back in time. In addition, hearths from such structures not only might yield radiocarbon dates but could be sampled to extend and refine the regional archaeomagnetic chronology.

Research Issue 2.2: Basketmaker II Subsistence

The record reveals that early maize from Durango area BMII sites expresses characteristics of a variety of maize types (Jones and Fonner 1954:111). Documented characteristics include the higher row numbers, starch caps, denting, and pyramidal cob shape of Mexican Pyramidal; the lower row numbers, row pairing, grooved cobs, flaring butts, and large shanks of Eastern types; and possibly even some Tropical Flint traits. Clearly, early BMII maize encompassed a surprising diversity that may reflect multiple or heterogeneous strains. In examining BMII subsistence in Ridges Basin, we will focus on (1) the degree of dependence on maize

through time, (2) the diversity of maize varieties through time, and (3) the possible relationship between these two factors. Fortunately, chronological analysis of maize is highly practicable, because any cob fragment or kernel that is large enough for morphological studies is also large enough for AMS dating.

Of particular interest is whether maize was as important in early BMII times as it evidently became after A.D. 1. As Lipe (1999) has noted,

> i[I]f maize was introduced by San Pedro–related colonists from farther south, it is likely that these settlers were already dependent on this crop. In this scenario, populations would have remained small and scattered because initially the introduced maize was not well adapted to the Four Corners area and could be grown only in a limited number of environmental settings (Matson 1991). On the other hand, if maize was adopted by indigenous farmers [as has been suggested for the Durango area in particular], it could either have rapidly become important, or it could have been used for a long time as a supplemental food source [Lipe 1999:164)].

Specific questions to address are: (1) When do cultigens appear in the project area and how soon after are groups fairly dependent on them? (2) Are there changes in the ground stone assemblage, and if so, when do these occur? (3) Do site locations reflect a dependence on agriculture or wild resources? (4) Are structures more substantial, and are storage features added to the inventory?

As Lipe (1999:165) indicated, understanding BMII dependence on maize is a key to understanding BMII subsistence in general. For example, did population growth in late BMII times eventually force groups to relegate foraging to a fallback role, setting in motion a greater dependence on dry farming and long-term storage of maize? Were these changes set off by the introduction or development of new varieties of maize and the beginnings of successful bean cultivation? Did warfare or some other social process promote a reduction in foraging and a commitment to greater dependence on stored maize, new land-tenure systems, and stronger communities?

Research Issue 2.3: Cultural Origins, Interregional Relationships, and Abandonment

To address Matson's (1991) proposal that Durango area BMII groups developed locally as a result of Late Archaic foragers adopting maize farming by diffusion, SWCA will conduct systematic comparisons of early BMII and Late Archaic complexes in the area to determine the degree of similarity (or difference) between the two. As part of the project's synthetic efforts, systematic comparisons of assemblages from eastern and western parts of the region may help determine if a cultural boundary exists between them.

Specific questions to address are: (1) Do Archaic and BMII sites overlap in time? (2) Are they situated in the same or different ecological niches? (3) Is there evidence, such as an increase in a particular projectile point style, for intrusive populations?

Like those from the Archaic period, BMII lithic assemblages often consist of a wide variety of stone materials from non-local sources. In addition, BMII sites frequently contain ornaments made of exotic materials such as shell. Identifying the sources of these materials and how they made their way into BMII sites will allow inferences regarding the direction and intensity of inter-areal relations, either through direct movement across the landscape (mobility) or through exchange with other groups. Projectile point styles might also inform us about the cultural affiliations of the Ridges Basin BMII groups and the direction of their social interactions. Establishing the direction and intensity of inter-areal relations through time is critical for understanding a group's cultural-historical connections, why a group left an area when it did, and where the people went when they left, and may help to address Lipe's (1999:165) question, "Did BMII groups maintain wide networks of trading partnerships to facilitate rapid movement into different areas if crops failed and local resources were inadequate?"

Assessing local environmental conditions during the late BMII period is also essential for understanding the abandonment of the area. Did the decrease in effective moisture circa A.D. 250 force the abandonment of Ridges Basin, or were forest clearing for maize farming, soil depletion, and over-hunting among the factors that encouraged groups to leave? Was social conflict an issue? Is there evidence of violence in BMII settlements, or of defensive structures such as stockades in the project area during this time, or are stockades solely a Basketmaker III phenomenon (Chenault and Motsinger 2000)?

By taking a long-term historical approach to the Archaic and Basketmaker occupations of the Ridges Basin area, looking at environmental changes, demographic and settlement organization changes, subsistence changes, and affiliation trends through time, it will be possible to reconstruct the particular trajectory of the Ridges Basin area hunter-gatherers and develop a well-documented study of early agricultural adaptations in the northern Southwest. It may then be possible to compare this historical case study to research in other areas of the world and contribute significantly to general cultural evolutionary models of the transition from a hunting and gathering lifeway to an agricultural lifeway.

Problem Domain 3: The Early Puebloan Occupation

Whereas the Archaic to Basketmaker occupation of the Ridges Basin area is an example of, and potential case study in, long-term historical development and locality abandonment, the early Pueblo I (PI) occupation (A.D. 750–825) is an unusual opportunity to examine one (or some) of the earliest communities in the Southwest during a highly restricted time span. SWCA's main interest is characterizing household and community organization in the area so that meaningful comparisons can be made with other areas, such as the Dolores area. In this way, variation that cannot be accounted for by environmental and demographic variables can be investigated in terms of cultural and historical factors. Actually quantifying this variation may allow for insights into the history of Ridges Basin area Puebloan groups, that is, where they came from, and where they went when they left the area.

For this research domain, SWCA will also investigate (1) site structure and settlement, (2) subsistence, (3) local and regional population growth and abandonment, (4) mobility-sedentism and land use, and (5) patterns of social and economic organization. These larger questions will be posed with regard to four scales of analysis: the household, the household cluster, the community, and the region.

Research Issue 3.1: The Pueblo I Household

A household is defined as a group of individuals who share a single residence and who cooperate on a regular basis in a number of basic economic and social activities. Households are thus defined primarily in terms of what they do rather than by kin relations among household members, providing a more effective basis for the comparative analysis of household organization (Varien 1999:16–17). Based on Lightfoot's (1994) work at the Duckfoot Site, a PI hamlet in the Mesa Verde region, we expect that the architectural expression of the household for PI sites in Ridges Basin is the individual pit structure and its associated surface rooms. Thus, the "unit pueblo" (the recurring association of a pit structure or kiva, a room block, and a trash area [Prudden 1903]) is interpreted as the archaeological correlate of the household. This, however, is an empirical issue that will be addressed in this research (see below).

Most of the PI households in Ridges Basin appear to date to the interval A.D. 750–825. The primary issues related to these roughly contemporaneous households are (1) dating their occupation more precisely, (2) determining their composition, and (3) identifying their organization.

Dates of Occupation

Based on the UMTRA excavations in nearby Bodo Canyon (Fuller 1988b), excavations north of Durango by Earl Morris (Ahlstrom 1985; Carlson 1963), excavations south of Durango by Gooding (1980), excavations on Blue Mesa for MAPCO (Fetterman and Honeycutt 1982), and ceramic data collected from Ridges Basin by NAU (Allison 1995), the PI occupation of the area was between A.D. 750 and 825. Assessing how individual households fit into this date range is fundamental to understanding their economic and social organization. Refining ceramic chronologies, recovering tree-ring samples, and obtaining radiocarbon and archaeomagnetic samples from individual structures will be important research goals. In addition to determining construction and use dates, however, SWCA is concerned with establishing the occupation duration of households so that their temporal overlap can be refined as much as possible.

We propose to address this issue from two perspectives: what might be termed a *relative* perspective, and an *absolute* perspective. The relative perspective simply ranks the households in the project area in terms of their relative occupation duration, based on the accumulation of associated artifacts, stratigraphy and remodeling data, and the range of dates from datable materials. This method will be useful in identifying major differences among household clusters or even communities in terms of the occupation duration of the households comprising them (see below). The absolute method, on the other hand, requires that each depositional context in each household (or at least the associated midden) be sampled randomly and an artifact population proportion be estimated so that the total accumulation of artifacts (e.g., cooking-pot sherds) per household can be quantified. These values can then be compared directly to discard rates calculated for the Duckfoot Site, a completely excavated, well-dated PI hamlet with an established use-life. From these comparisons a probable occupation date range can be calculated for each household sampled (Lightfoot 1994; Varien and Mills 1997; Varien and Potter 1997). This information is important for understanding and quantifying the overall variability of household occupation duration and is critical to establishing momentary population estimates within the project area, as well as understanding the process by which the area was initially populated and ultimately depopulated (e.g., by individual households over time or by larger groups more or less at once).

Refined chronological controls are also important for assessing models of occupation and abandonment of various regions during the PI period. For example, Schlanger and Wilshusen (1993) suggested that PI residential mobility patterns correspond to intensified drought conditions; during periods of lower-than-average effective moisture, what they term "run for your life" (RFYL) periods, construction ceases in the Dolores area, and they interpret these as episodes of abandonment. RFYL periods are countered by "don't worry be happy" (DWBH) periods in which effective moisture is average or above average and in which construction dates cluster.

Based on data from the Dolores Archaeological Project (DAP), the RFYL drought periods that may be relevant to the Ridges Basin area occupation span the intervals from A.D. 740 to 760 (the assumed beginning of occupation in Ridges Basin) and A.D. 810 to 830 (the assumed end of the Ridges Basin occupation) (Schlanger and Wilshusen 1993:89). Timing construction episodes and the abandonment of individual households relative to these 20-year intervals will be the key step in understanding the effects of drought on mobility patterns and household- and community-level decision-making. SWCA will be particularly concerned with similarities or differences in response to drought conditions, both among various clusters of households in the project area and in comparison to those in Dolores communities. Variation within the project area and from the Dolores pattern may signal cultural-historical differences in terms of decision structures and household and community organization.

Household Composition and Organization

A household is defined in terms of the activities that it conducts, including those associated with production, reproduction, exchange, subsistence, and ritual. Specific questions regarding household composition and organization are: (1) What is the architectural expression of the early PI household in the Durango area? (2) Does each household perform the same range of activities, or is there some level of socio-economic interdependence among households within a household cluster or community? (3) What do surface rooms represent functionally? (4) Are all pit structures domestic in nature, or are ritual attributes associated with some? (5) What do micro-artifacts associated with room floors tell us about the function and use of those rooms?

Debate over the architectural composition of the PI household emerged as a result of DAP and the Crow Canyon Archaeological Center's (CCAC's) excavations at the Duckfoot Site in southwestern Colorado. Work conducted as part of DAP in the 1980s suggested that multiple households occupied surface room suites and shared a pit structure. The evidence that led to this conclusion was primarily architectural in nature—surface room suites tended to be segregated by a lack of connecting doorways between them, suggesting a segregation of activities and restricted social interaction (Kane 1986). Following DAP, which sampled a number of large sites, CCAC intensively excavated one PI hamlet containing four pit structures and associated surface

rooms and concluded that, instead of each pit structure and its associated rooms representing two to three nuclear families sharing a pit house, the unit centered on the pit structure and housed one extended family (Lightfoot 1994). Aboveground facilities were interpreted, based primarily on artifact distributions and activity segregation, as having become more substantial and specialized to allow more storage of surpluses and more privacy for individuals. The practical consequence of this distinction is that population estimates are significantly lower if just one extended family occupied a pit structure unit.

The main reason this debate emerged in the first place was the apparent contrast between the typical Basketmaker III (BMIII) and PI residential suites in the Dolores area. BMIII (A.D. 500–750) sites consisted of a shallow pit structure and several shallow, isolated storage structures, or pit rooms, and are thought to have represented a single household. PI sites in this area contained deeper pit structures and suites of contiguous aboveground domestic and storage rooms. This change is often referred to as the pit house to pueblo transition, and in the DAP model signaled a change in social organization from single- to multiple-household occupation of unit pueblos.

Importantly, the transition to more substantial aboveground rooms during the PI period did not occur in the Durango area. In fact, one of the striking patterns in the Ridges Basin area is the ephemeral nature of surface rooms at PI sites (Fuller 1988b; Gooding 1980). As noted above, in the Dolores area ephemeral surface rooms tend to be associated with BMIII sites, which has led some researchers (e.g., Gooding 1980) to refer to sites in the Durango area dating solidly to the PI period (A.D. 750–825) as BMIII. Surface room architecture has not been well investigated in the Ridges Basin area because of poor preservation, so the ALP project offers a unique opportunity to investigate morphology, construction techniques, and function in PI surface architecture in the Durango area. Identifying use surfaces and sampling them for micro-artifacts, including micro-debitage, very small faunal remains, and pollen, can be an effective strategy for characterizing activities within a room (Chenault 2002). Documenting variation in surface room architecture and the activities that occurred within rooms will be important for understanding household organization differences and trends, as well as site populations, within the project area. We expect that the architectural expression of the household is the pit structure and its associated surface rooms and other extramural features. Pit structures in the Durango area appear to occur individually with room blocks. No excavated sites have contained more than one pit structure per room block, further suggesting that the pit structure was the center of a single household. Six of the larger habitation sites in Ridges Basin may contain two pit structure depressions. Subsurface investigations will be required to confirm the presence of multiple pit structures and the model of household organization proposed here.

Pit structures in the Ridges Basin area appear to have a suite of floor, bench, and roof-support features similar to that in PI pit structures in other areas. Functional interpretations of pit structures range from purely domestic to ritual. Lightfoot (1994:148–149) has argued in the case of the Duckfoot Site, a PI hamlet, that both pit structures and room blocks were used by households as residential space, in contrast to the evidence from villages, where some "over-sized" pit structures were clearly used by multiple households for community activities (Wilshusen 1989). It is unclear whether the central village, Site 5LP245, contains any over-sized pit structures or possibly even a great kiva, but most pit structures in the project area are expected to have been used primarily as domestic living space.

Artifact, micro-artifact, and feature data all have the potential to yield information on the range of activities conducted in pit structures. It is particularly important to establish these pit structure functional differences within and among sites when (1) documenting household organization within a community and (2) estimating site or regional population levels, which often use the number of *domestic* pit structures as a proxy measure of site population. With this in mind, and given the ephemeral nature of surface architecture in the area, SWCA will be particularly interested in measuring the ratio of domestic to ritual activities in pit structures and addressing differences in organization of activities within pit structures in Ridges Basin relative to other areas, such as the Dolores area. Is the organization of activities within the Ridges Basin unit pueblo more similar to what has been found in other areas, such as the upper San Juan Basin, than in the Dolores area? If so, why might this be the case? Do oversized pit structures, if present, appear to have functioned differently in the Ridges Basin area than they did in the Dolores area? If so, what accounts for this variation?

Extramural features are important components of households as well. These features can define not only the activities associated with a household but also the spatial boundaries of the household. Enclosures constructed of posts, low adobe walls, or cobble aprons are especially important for defining space around residences in the Durango area. Enclosures of some form have been shown to be part of early PI sites on Blue Mesa and in Bodo Canyon (Horn et al. 2003; Fuller 1988b). Some early PI sites in Hidden Valley, just north of Durango, also had enclosures (Carlson 1963). These features tend to surround the pit house, surface rooms, and extramural features and unambiguously define extramural space for the household. Middens are sometimes located outside the enclosure. SWCA will employ extensive mechanical stripping to document the presence, extent, and construction methods of enclosures in the project area. Other extramural features that may be exposed through careful stripping are hearths, pits, roasting pits, and burials. Prudent use of both hand and mechanical excavation will allow SWCA to effectively document the variation in and organization of activities associated with households.

Production and Exchange

Two of the most important activities that households participate in are production and exchange of material items. Recent studies suggest that ceramic production throughout the Southwest was often specialized at a relatively low level, with variation in the ratio of producing to non-producing households and in the degree to which producers were spatially clustered. Most ceramics were made at the household level, but not every household made enough pottery to meet its needs. Some households produced only certain kinds of pottery, or none at all, and acquired from others what they did not make themselves. Although variation in producer/consumer ratios and spatial distribution of producers is continuous, it is useful to think in terms of three modes of production: (1) unspecialized production, in which every household produces enough to meet its own needs; (2)

dispersed specialization, in which ceramic-producing households are distributed evenly across the landscape, producing pottery for their own needs and those of their non-producing neighbors; and (3) community or regional specialization, in which ceramic producers are spatially clustered into one or more communities and trade their surplus to consumers living in different communities.

Previous studies in the Dolores area have found ware-specific patterns of ceramic production as well as temporal variation in those patterns (Blinman 1986, 1988; Blinman and Wilson 1988; Wilson and Blinman 1995a). Prior to A.D. 800, grayware production was widespread but not ubiquitous, while whiteware production was more specialized. Thus, a majority of households in the Dolores area, but probably not all, produced grayware, while a much smaller number of households produced whiteware. During the latter part of the PI period, after A.D. 840, grayware ceramics were probably produced in every household or interhousehold group in the Dolores area, while whiteware production continued to be specialized. Redware production was thought to be regionally specialized, with all redwares found in Dolores-area sites originating in southeastern Utah. There is little evidence on the spatial distribution of whiteware producers in the Dolores area, but regional variation in whiteware pigments and designs suggests that whiteware producers were more dispersed than redware producers.

Similar complexity in ceramic production is expected among PI households in Ridges Basin. Documenting those patterns will be important in understanding variability (or lack thereof) in the activities of different households, as well as interaction among households. Ceramic production evidence in the form of kilns, raw materials (unfired clays, pigments, or temper), and pottery-making tools (scrapers or polishing stones) in excavated collections will provide information on the number and spatial distribution of pottery-producing households.

Preliminary studies of pottery from Ridges Basin have demonstrated variability in the clays and tempers used to make both graywares and whitewares (Allison 1995). Grayware sherds in particular oxidized to a wide variety of colors, suggesting that many different clay sources

were used. There are several possible reasons for this variation in tempers and clays, but whatever the cause, it should be possible to use it to infer patterns of interactions among households, although detailed study will be required to determine the precise nature of the interactions. By implication, many different potters were involved in producing the ceramics found in Ridges Basin, but it is unclear how much of the pottery was produced there. Pottery made from different clays may reflect different choices by potters within Ridges Basin, or perhaps by potters in Ridges Basin and on Blue Mesa. It may also indicate that a relatively high proportion of the ceramics used in Ridges Basin was made in surrounding areas.

To resolve these issues, SWCA will attempt to document the sources of the raw materials used in ceramic production as specifically as possible using several methods. Binocular examination of temper, thin-section analysis, and oxidation studies of recovered ceramics will be combined with attempts to locate potential clay and temper sources in Ridges Basin and surrounding areas.

In the ideal case, spatial variation would be found that could be used to infer that ceramics with certain clays or tempers were made in different parts of the project area. If so, the distribution of ceramics made with these raw materials outside of their production areas should indicate fairly direct interaction with the households that produced them. However, given the small size of Ridges Basin, it may not be possible to segregate ceramics made in different parts of the basin. If clay-resource surveys suggest that most of the pottery was made there, any differences in oxidized colors would probably reflect the use of different clay recipes or sources within the basin, even if these differences were not based on geographic residence. Instead, they would most likely reflect learning traditions and hence interactions among potters, with potters tending to use the raw materials used by their teachers and close associates. The distributions of ceramics made with different clays or clay recipes should thus reflect patterns of interaction among pottery-making households and between producing and non-producing households.

Finally, if most of the variation turns out to indicate importation of ceramics from a variety of sources outside the project area, the distribution of pottery made from different clays and tempers would then indicate interaction between households within Ridges Basin and ceramic producers in other areas. Interactions among households within the project area could still be inferred, however, as similarity in the kinds of imported pottery can be used to identify households that maintained similar exchange networks (see Allison 2000).

Bioarchaeological Signatures of Production

The degree to which individual members of PI period households participated in ceramic production will be evaluated through observation of skeletal markers of occupation stress (Kennedy 1983, 1989, 1998). Differences in the nature and intensity of ceramic manufacturing processes produce different skeletal signatures relating to robusticity and symmetry in the bones of the upper limb. For example, Perry (2004) has connected fifth metacarpal ligament site asymmetry in women to intensive ceramic manufacture. Documenting patterns of musculo-skeletal stress markers characteristic of the biomechanical impact of the various stages of pottery production will enable ALP researchers to determine (1) the relative participation of males, females, and individuals of different ages in ceramic manufacture and (2) if differences exist in the intensity of such labor across different households. .

Seasonality

Winter et al. (1986) identified a pattern in Ridges Basin in which upland PI habitation sites generally appeared to be smaller and less clustered than lowland sites. Ware (1986) proposed that these patterns are the result of seasonality—upland sites were used in the winter, and lowland sites were occupied during the spring, summer, and fall. SWCA will explore this possibility by documenting through excavation how consistent the size distinction is, how substantial the occupations appear to have been, and how specialized the artifact assemblages are in upland versus lowland sites. SWCA will also systematically collect charred plant and faunal data that may shed light on seasonality at both upland and lowland sites.

Research Issue 3.2: The Household Cluster and the Community

Although multiple-household room blocks may be relatively rare in the Ridges Basin area, spatial clusters of household units do appear on the landscape. Fuller (1989) identifies nine such clusters within the project area, eight within Ridges Basin and one on Blue Mesa (Figure 3).

What these clusters represent socially and economically remains to be explored. Assuming rough contemporaneity among household clusters, several important question arise: (1) Do these clusters represent villages? (2) Is the placement of clusters on the landscape structured by environmental or catchment variables (e.g., arable land and water) or by social variables (such as proximity to other clusters or defensibility concerns)? (3) Are all clusters similarly organized, or is there an organizational hierarchy? (4) Is there another level of organization above the cluster?

We agree with Lekson (1991:42) that "if the unit house is the fundamental element of Anasazi architecture, the community is the fundamental unit of Anasazi settlement." This is especially true for the Mesa Verde region, where archaeological survey has consistently shown that residential sites do not occur in isolation but rather are grouped together into settlement clusters (Varien 1999). Given that settlement is clustered at a number of inclusive levels, which level of settlement clustering represents a community?

We define a community as a spatially delimited group of people who interact on a fairly intensive and regular basis (see Murdock 1949). As Varien (1999:19–20) has pointed out, a community possesses temporal, spatial, and social dimensions. The temporal and spatial aspects are fairly straightforward: people must live at least some of the time in relative proximity in order to interact on a regular basis.

The social dimension arises from the fact that community members share in access to local material resources, such as land and hunted game, as well as social resources, such as labor and communal rituals. Thus, a community may consist of hamlets or villages dispersed across a landscape, as long as the defined criteria are met. A fundamental question then is whether the clusters in Ridges Basin form a number of small individual communities or one or more large ones. It will also be important to compare the Ridges Basin clusters to the very large one on Blue Mesa, which comprises up to 50 households. The eight clusters in Ridges Basin are demonstrably smaller, with a mean of eight household units. One of these clusters, though, contains a village-sized aggregate (with more than 15 pit structures) in addition to dispersed hamlet units.

Given the available information, at least three types of community organization appear to be possible for Ridges Basin. The first possibility is that Ridges Basin and Blue Mesa together make up one large, complex community, with the Ridges Basin community dispersed in multiple sub-community clusters. The second is that Ridges Basin and Blue Mesa are the loci of two distinct communities, possibly contemporaneous. The Ridges Basin community would have been more dispersed, with a large village at its core. The third possibility is that Ridges Basin and Blue Mesa are examples of Lipe's (1994) concept of "first-order, face-to-face communities," which might be analogous to Fuller's clusters. One feature of the first-order communities model is that they can form alliances with other, similar communities, but that the alliances are conceptually distinct from the communities themselves. Lipe further argues that these supra-community alliances need not exhibit formal political hierarchy or a regional polity, which implies that they may not be as persistent through time as the first-order communities that constitute them. To assess these three possible community organization models, SWCA will collect data related to three important social and economic dimensions: population, interaction, and interdependence (or integration).

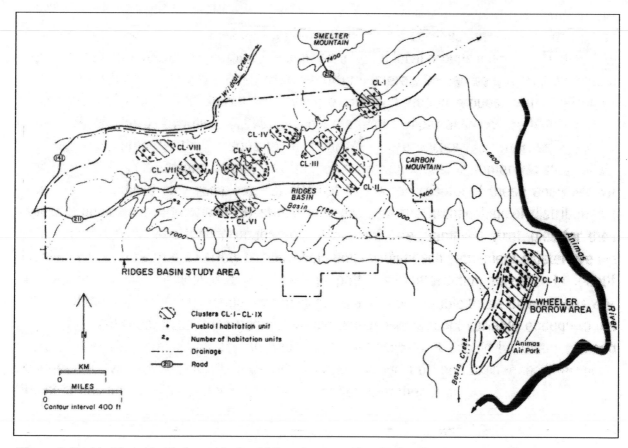

Figure 3. Pueblo I household clusters in the ALP project area (from Fuller 1989).

Momentary Population Levels

Based on a Monte Carlo simulation, Wobst (1974) suggested that human mating networks among Paleolithic hunters and gatherers require a face-to-face population of 175 to 475 individuals to ensure that everyone can find a non-related marriage partner. More recently, Mahoney (1998) has argued that the conservative figure of 475 might be close to the minimum size for a horticultural community. This number may be too high, however, and a more realistic minimum population size may be around 150–200. In any case, these figures suggest that the simple need to establish marriage alliances among dispersed horticulturalists may account for the tendency of early Puebloan habitation units to cluster in space.

Cross-cultural research indicates that there is also an upper limit to the population of communities in politically non-stratified societies. In a worldwide sample that included examples from the American Southwest, Adler (1990, 1994; Adler and Varien 1994) found that such communities do not exceed 1,500 people. Thus, there are population thresholds as well as spatial thresholds that can help define the upper limits for the size of Mesa Verde–region communities. Establishing momentary populations within Ridges Basin during the PI period will be of primary concern to SWCA researchers and may aid in determining the spatial scale of "community" in the Durango area.

The demographic composition of the skeletal population from Ridges Basin will provide an indication of the level of stress experienced by these communities. The biocultural concept of stress provides a framework for assessing the overall stability of the population, their susceptibility to disruptive events, and their health status (Goodman et al. 1988). Documentation of infant mortality, incidence of disease and infection, achieved stature, and dental pathology in the Ridges Basin skeletal series will provide a detailed picture of the degree to which certain stresses impacted these communities.

Interaction among Households

Some of the best tools for measuring interaction involve ceramic sourcing. Both clay and temper can often be traced to their geologic sources. If local groups used different sources for either of these resources when making pottery, interaction can be quantified based on how much of a given material was being exchanged between different groups. Initial refiring of Ridges Basin sherds by Allison (1995) suggests that both temper and clay vary widely from site to site, although the reasons for this variation are unclear. To address this issue, SWCA proposes to (1) conduct clay and temper source analyses on numerous sherds (and, if found, on unfired clay samples), (2) attempt to link the results of these analyses with specific geologic sources, and (3) statistically evaluate the archaeological distribution of sourced sherds vis-à-vis their probable loci of manufacture. Sampling strategies for these studies will ensure representation of a variety of household units within each settlement cluster. If the geology is distinct enough, patterns of interaction may then be identifiable, and it may be possible to establish the nature of interaction among clusters and how these interactions may have varied. Even if the geology within Ridges Basin is too homogeneous to indicate patterns of interaction among household unit clusters, there should be enough difference between Ridges Basin and Blue Mesa to address differences in production and exchange in these areas and assess patterns of interaction between them.

Another method for evaluating interaction among household clusters is to quantify household ceramic assemblage functional attributes, such as proportions of different pottery forms and wares, in order to derive inferences about range and intensity of behaviors. For instance, Blinman (1989) documented an inverse relationship in the proportion of redware serving bowls and grayware cooking vessels among households within McPhee Village. He attributed this pattern to the spatial disjunction between food preparation behaviors (cooking in grayware jars) and food consumption behaviors (serving in redware bowls) and suggests that potluck-style feasting (and inter-household interaction) was occurring in the large village. Allison (1995) notes that redware sherds are rare in Ridges Basin surface assemblages, especially at larger habitation sites. Excavation data are needed to corroborate this pattern, but it suggests that redware bowls and the behaviors associated with them were not as important here as they were in the Dolores area. However, other ceramic wares/types may have served similar functions in this area, or communal behaviors may have been organized differently or involved a different range of activities.

A third measure that SWCA will use to assess levels of interaction is the distribution and exchange of large game within the project area as a whole or between Ridges Basin and Blue Mesa. If certain anatomical portions of large game are proportionately more common in some clusters of household units, and other anatomical portions are more common in other clusters, consistent exchange of animal portions, as seen in other PI communities (Potter 1997), may account for this pattern.

Interdependence of Households

SWCA will pursue several measures of interdependence (or community integration) among household clusters. These measures fall into two categories: the *complementarity* of resource access and production behaviors, and the *shared use* of resources, both environmental and social.

Resource and Activity Complementarity

Use of resource and activity complementarity as a measure of interdependence is based on the idea that certain households or household clusters have access to particular resources and/or produce certain items that complement those of other households, thereby encouraging interaction, or at least exchange, among groups. Indicators of complementarity may be related to agricultural productivity, wild resource availability, and production of pottery, tools, and other goods.

The agricultural potential of soils in the project area varies widely due to a number of factors, including aspect, elevation, the types of bedrock outcrops exposed, and soil quality and quantity. Fuller (1989:79) suggested that the size or scale of a community should be directly correlated with the productivity of the agricultural catchment surrounding that community. A lack of correlation between community scale and agricultural catchment may imply some sort of functional differentiation at the community level.

According to preliminary analyses, only two clusters within the ALP project are in areas with high agricultural potential (Fuller 1989:64); one is the Blue Mesa cluster. Five clusters are in soils with moderate potential, and one—the largest in Ridges Basin, containing Site 5LP245—is associated with low-potential soils that extend in a 0.5-km radius. This distribution suggests the possibility that some clusters were more active in agricultural production than others and that some food-sharing interdependence existed among the clusters.

SWCA will conduct detailed catchment analyses of both domesticated and wild resources around each cluster, using both systematic on-the-ground observations and GIS. Four strategies will be employed to assess the spatial variation of plants and soils within the basin and determine catchment values. The first step will be detailed geomorphic analysis of soils within the project area and production of a detailed soils map for use in a GIS analysis. The second step will be a complete plant inventory and preparation of a plant-community distribution map that will be linked with the soil map. Using the method outlined in Adams (1978), individual plant types will be ranked based on their potential economic returns and abundance across the landscape, and economic values will be assigned to definable areas within the basin. Third, experimental dry-farm gardens will be placed across the basin at various elevations and aspects to assess variation in growing potential. The multi-year aspect of this project will also allow an assessment of the correlation between variations in precipitation from year to year and garden productivity. And fourth, we will establish computerized weather stations in the garden plots to measure precipitation, soil moisture, wind, and temperature for a number of years to assess these variables within the basin, from season to season and year to year.

If agricultural production (relative to population) was distributed unevenly among clusters, then we might expect storage to be distributed unevenly as well. Quantifying storage space relative to living space within household clusters will help to evaluate whether some clusters were more agriculturally productive than others. Surface-room area may be the best measure of storage space because of the supposed storage function of these structures. This association remains to be demonstrated, however.

Uneven distribution of other resources among clusters may signal a certain level of economic interdependence. At McPhee Village, for example, distributions of faunal taxa were highly patterned; the assemblage from one large household cluster was dominated by artiodactyls, while another was heavily dominated by lagomorphs

(Potter 1997). This complementarity of seasonally acquired faunal resources may relate to larger community economic dynamics, such as the division of the "hunting year" among household clusters. Do some households appear to have had more access to long-distance hunted resources, such as large game, while others focused more on garden hunting?

Finally, variation in the distribution of production activities related to pottery, lithic artifacts, bone tools, or other goods may also have promoted greater interdependence among household units. Blinman (1988) noted that pottery production tools and raw materials (unfired clays and tempers) within Dolores PI villages were not clustered to the point of indicating that pottery production was centralized, or even involved specialists, but he also noted that not every household made pottery, suggesting some level of interdependence on the part of households. Since agricultural productivity was apparently so patchy within Ridges Basin, it is possible that pottery production was a way for some households to hedge against this resource deficiency and participate in a system of interdependence. One hypothesis that would account for the siting of the largest PI site in Ridges Basin, 5LP245, in an area of low agricultural potential is that it specialized in pottery rather than agriculture. This would also account for the low proportion at the site, relative to local wares, of redwares, which may not have been locally made. SWCA will make every effort to recover evidence of pottery production from each household unit investigated and compare the distribution of these data to other economic data within and among clusters. The distribution of PI limited-activity, non-habitation sites on the landscape may also aid in assessing the consistency of the range of activities actually conducted by members of each household unit cluster.

Shared Resources

Documenting the shared use of resources also has the potential to illuminate other aspects of communities within Ridges Basin. One of the more significant breakthroughs in the last 15 years has been understanding the role that public architecture plays in the integration of households into communities in small-scale agricultural societies (Adler 1989; Adler and Varien 1994; Lipe and Hegmon 1989; Varien 1999). Identifying shared architectural space in which communal-integrative activities occurred is key to defining a community. Studies by Adler (1989) and Adler and Wilshusen (1990) indicate that public structures used by entire communities tend to have the largest floor areas and the most specialized uses of any buildings in the community. These cross-cultural patterns help us identify particular buildings in the Mesa Verde region as public architecture. In Ridges Basin, the nature and abundance of public architecture is unclear. Site 5LP245 contains possible public architecture in the form of at least one oversized pit structure and/or a plaza. SWCA will assess the nature of these features by re-excavating them. We will also investigate, through excavation, whether other oversized pit structures exist in Ridges Basin and, if so, their relationship to the habitation clusters. In addition to their larger size, these features are expected to yield artifact, faunal, and feature evidence of a range of ritual and feasting activities (Blinman 1989; Potter 1997, 2000; Wilshusen 1989).

Shared burial grounds can also indicate levels of integration above the household unit cluster. A distributional study of burial location and basic composition may add substantial information to community-oriented studies.

One topic that deserves greater attention than it has received in the past is conflict and defense. Are households clustered for defense purposes, and, if so, what does this tell us about interactions among these clusters? Martin and Goodman (1995) have documented traumatic lesions and associated pathologies on a number of human skeletons recovered from Ridges Basin. Assessing the distribution, causes, and pervasiveness of skeletal evidence of violence will help determine the ultimate causal effect of these behaviors on settlement patterns and interaction among household clusters. Defensive architecture provides other evidence of possible conflict. Chenault and Motsinger (2000) document a number of BMIII hamlets with associated protective stockades in the Mesa Verde region. These features are also common in early PI sites to the south of the project area. SWCA's field methods will include extensive excavations to recover any available data on defensive architecture. The temporal and spatial distribution of any defensive structures that are present will provide information on the pervasiveness of conflict and the nature of relationships among household clusters.

The Sacred Ridge Site

Site 5LP245, also known as the Sacred Ridge Site, is a PI (A.D. 700–850) village at the west end of Ridges Basin. As the name suggests, the site occupies the top and sides of a small ridge. The latest recordation of the site by NAU mapped 10 room block units (Morris 1995) (Figure 4). Each of these units comprises at least one pit structure and a series of surface rooms. The extent of subsurface remains at the site is likely much greater than the surface evidence indicates. We estimate that 10 to 15 pit structures and their associated surface architecture

remain to be excavated on the eastern and western flanks of the ridge.

The site has been a favorite of local artifact collectors and looters for nearly a century. Homer Root, who directed the Fort Lewis College field school in the 1960s, noted that "as many as fifty people might be counted on the site during a week-end, searching and digging for relics" (Root 1967:12). The site was officially recorded in 1975 (Leidy 1976), and subsequently rerecorded by ESCA-Tech (Winter et al. 1986), CASA (SHPO site card updates only), and NAU (Morris 1995). Each recordation of the site involved some type of surface collection. The largest and most systematic was by NAU and included comprehensive mapping of the site.

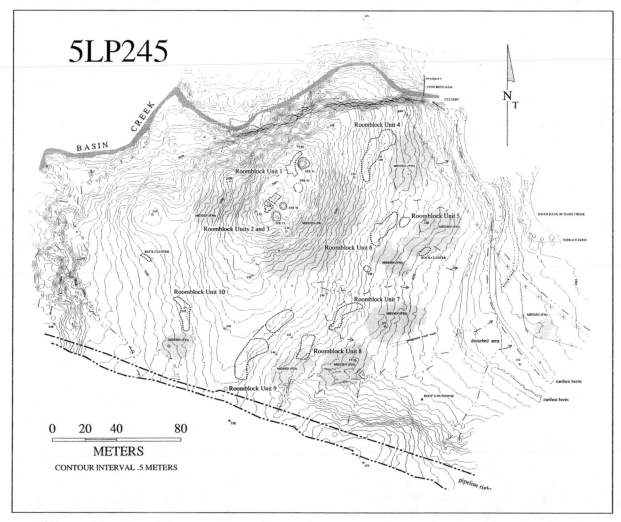

Figure 4. Map of the Sacred Ridge Site (5LP245), compliments of James N. Morris.

The Fort Lewis College field school conducted excavations at the site under the direction of Homer Root in 1966 and 1967 (see Root 1967). It was at this time that the site was first referred to as "Sacred Ridge" in the literature. These excavations were marginally controlled and poorly documented—a hand-written journal kept by Root is the only existing record. Whether any of the students kept notes on their excavations is not clear. Root's journal includes unscaled drawings of artifacts, burials, and structures in a style reminiscent of late nineteenth century archaeologists. A handful of 35-mm slides and a short 16-mm film are the only existing photographic documentation. Most of the slides and a large portion of the film appear to have been taken on the same day, at the end of the 1966 field season.

It is evident from Root's journal that his primary interest was in acquiring interesting "specimens" for the Fort Lewis College museum. Only whole or unique artifacts were collected, and no samples of any kind. Some of the artifacts were arranged in mosaics for presentation (see Duke 1985:122–123). Burials were sought out for their grave goods; the human remains were not analyzed until decades later (see Martin and Goodman 1995). Unfortunately, a large portion of the Root collection from Sacred Ridge is missing entirely.

The 1966 field school investigated the deposits on top of the ridge and the trash deposits on the lower slopes of 5LP245. Root's journal records the excavation of three pit structures, two "dance areas," 28 surface rooms, and 40 human burials (Root 1967). SWCA will re-explore this area and attempt to re-document the work that Root conducted and recover any additional information from this area of the site. The descriptions of unique features in Root's notes suggest that this area may have been an important ritual area for the village and perhaps for the entire basin.

In addition, SWCA will excavate the houses around the ridge top and assess to what degree they are similar to or different from houses in other site clusters in the project area. Several questions will be the focus of research. Are the houses associated with the village contemporaneous with the architecture on top of the ridge? Is the architecture associated with this site largely contemporaneous with other PI sites in Ridges Basin and Blue Mesa? What is the range of variation among the Sacred

Ridge Site houses? Are they morphologically different from houses in other site clusters? Are they all purely domestic structures, or do some appear to have been the locus of ritual activities? Is there evidence that this site was the ritual center for the entire basin? Is there, for instance, evidence of communal feasting or communal ritual that is not evident elsewhere? Is a great kiva associated with the site? What other activities are evident at the Sacred Ridge Site that are not evident elsewhere? The site seems to be in an area of low agricultural productivity. If this is the case, what role did this site play in the larger Ridges Basin community? Is the burial population at this site unique in any way?

Because of the multi-scalar aspect of settlement clustering in the area and the potential to firmly establish contemporaneity among residential units, the ALP project has tremendous potential to add to our understanding of early Puebloan community organization in the Mesa Verde region. Analysis of this variability will be essential to a full understanding of Mesa Verde–region society, and of the societies that ultimately evolved from these cultural-historical patterns.

Settlement Aggregation

Several models will be explored to understand the processes of settlement aggregation in the project area. The first suggests that aggregation was a result of local population increase and a resultant shortage of agricultural land. Under this model, households are expected to have clustered near to but not on prime agricultural land. The model also expects a more dispersed pattern initially and more clustering through time, as population increases and the landscape fills up with people. Evaluating the distribution of highly productive soils and the placement and number of habitation sites will be crucial to evaluating this model.

The second model stipulates that the main cause of household aggregation was the presence of strong or charismatic leaders who encouraged households to cluster near them for a number of reasons, including protection, social status, and other social, ideological, and economic benefits that such associations could provide. This model expects (1) elaborate architecture and behaviors associated with the aggregate (i.e., competitive display), (2) aggregation at the outset of or quickly after initial occupation of the area rather than gradually through time, and (3) very large, tight aggregation (i.e., village aggregation). This scenario could be associated with increased violence, encouraging households to aggregate (though violence could certainly be a factor in aggregation independent of strong leadership).

The third model predicts that aggregation occurred as a result of the development of matrilocal residence rules. John Ware (2002) suggests that aggregation of households can happen when men move to live with their wives' families and need to maintain connections with and live close by kin groups as well. In this model, clustering of houses is a simple function of logistical efficiency in the face of adhering to certain residence rules. According to Ware, matrilocality arises most often in matrilineal endogamous communities. Skeletal data may allow for the reconstruction of relatedness and marriage and residence rules within and among clusters, and it may be possible to test this model with the ALP data. It is important to stress that these models are not mutually exclusive and that probably all played a part in encouraging aggregation. The goal will be to tease out the strongest and most important factors underlying the aggregation process.

Research Issue 3.3: Comparing Ridges Basin and Blue Mesa

One of the more exciting aspects of the ALP project is the opportunity to investigate two large, roughly adjacent areas of dense prehistoric occupation, Ridges Basin and Blue Mesa. Interesting differences exist between the two areas, including much better soils and much denser occupation on Blue Mesa. It has also been suggested that Blue Mesa may have been occupied slightly later than Ridges Basin. While the Blue Mesa sample will not be as complete as the Ridges Basin sample, general comparisons should be possible in terms of architectural variability, pottery production and exchange, agricultural and hunting practices, chronology and processes of abandonment, and chronology of occupation.

Fuller (1988a) posited that Blue Mesa served as a refugium for Durango Ancestral Puebloans, including Ridges Basin occupants, during the period from A.D. 800 to 830. To test this model, SWCA will conduct detailed chronological and abandonment studies at each

household unit excavated in Ridges Basin. Schlanger and Wilshusen (1993) model four abandonment strategies that vary with the distance of a residential move and whether the occupants anticipated returning to the abandoned sites. They used floor artifact assemblages and roof treatment at abandonment to determine which abandonment strategy characterized each of four abandonments in the Dolores Valley between A.D. 600 and 910. They conclude that the first three abandonments were short term and that reoccupation of the locality was anticipated. The last abandonment, in the late A.D. 800s, appeared to be part of a regional abandonment with no plan to return.

It is important to recognize that in Schlanger and Wilshusen's and model, drought might have caused the emigration of *communities,* but it was not the sole reason for abandonment of residential sites by *households.* Many residences were abandoned during episodes of increased moisture (Schlanger and Wilshusen 1993:94). In fact, PI households had a use-life of 15 to 25 years, while many PI communities lasted 25 to 40 years (Wilshusen 1999:232), so some abandonment of sites is to be expected within a community. Varien (1999) documents a similar pattern of household mobility within more persistent communities during the Pueblo II and Pueblo III periods in the Mesa Verde region. Thus, documenting whether Ridges Basin was abandoned in favor of Blue Mesa requires detailed abandonment studies examining whole communities, not just the few household units that have been examined thus far.

Research Issue 3.4: Cultural Origins, Interregional Relationships, and Abandonment of the Area

PI people in the Durango area appear to have been influenced by a number of different but contemporaneous culture groups. To the west, in the Mesa Verde region, some people made the early and full transition to surface habitation and built large room blocks with both habitation and storage rooms. Their pit houses tended to be square to rectangular in shape, with wingwalls in their southern halves. They produced pottery with crushed andesite-diorite temper (Allison 1995). Archaeologists term these attributes Piedra phase. Groups to the southeast, in the upper San Juan drainage and up into parts of the Durango area, apparently did not make the early transition to surface habitation. Surface rooms were often built entirely aboveground (leading to poor preservation) and often seem to have been used primarily for storage. Pit houses tended to be circular in plan, have bifurcated vent openings, and lack wingwalls. Groups in this area produced a pottery with crushed quartz-feldspar temper (Allison 1995). Sites with these attributes are classified as Rosa phase (Table 2, Figure 5).

Sites in the Durango area exhibit characteristics of both the Piedra and Rosa traditions, and perhaps others as well. Sites 5LP478 (Fuller 1988b), Ignacio 7:31 and 7:36 (Carlson 1963), and 5LP171 and 5LP245 (Duke 1985) contain multiple large room blocks that resemble those from the Piedra area, while at 5LP481 (Fuller 1988b), Ignacio 7:23 and 7:30 (Carlson 1963), and 5LP110 (Gooding 1980) the room blocks share similarities with Rosa area sites. The local ceramics also exhibit characteristics of both areas; they commonly contain either andesite-diorite temper or quartz-feldspar temper, or a combination of the two, and painted designs are often of the Piedra style (Allison 1995).

The cultural trait showing most variation in the Durango area, however, is pit structure morphology, including not just the size and shape of the structures but functional attributes as well, such as the presence or absence of benches, two-holed vents, a four-post roof support system, and so forth. Pit structure shape is particularly variable in the area, suggesting that more than one, and possibly more than two, ethnic or cultural groups occupied the area during the early PI period (Figure 6).

Several questions thus arise. How many different ethnic or cultural groups made up the PI population of Ridges Basin? Where did they come from? How did the geographical origin of various groups affect how they were organized on the landscape? Did certain groups arrive first? Were the occupants of the Sacred Ridge Site the earliest occupants of the area, and was their cultural make-up heterogeneous or homogeneous? What mechanisms were used to integrate a community of households from various cultural and ethnic backgrounds? And finally, what role did the Sacred Ridge Site play in this community integration?

To address three of these issues—(1) whether individuals recovered from burial contexts in the project area are non-local, (2) the number of non-local groups that resided in Ridges Basin during the PI period, and (3) where these groups originated—radiogenic isotope analysis will be conducted (Ezzo and Price 2002). This type of analysis measures strontium isotope ratios ($^{87}Sr/^{86}Sr$) in human molar enamel to document and compare provenance of human populations. To be effective, such an analysis requires movement of people between distinct geological provinces, as $^{87}Sr/^{86}Sr$ in the calcified tissues of an organism is a reflection of the geological province where that individual obtained food. The analysis compares the strontium signature of the enamel from the first molar, which forms in the first year of life and does not remodel afterward, with the signature in local faunal bone (particularly of rodents or animals with very restricted ranges), which provides a baseline for local variation. If, for example, an individual buried at a site has an $^{87}Sr/^{86}Sr$ in the first molar enamel that is significantly different than the local signature, it can be inferred that this person is non-local and may have migrated from a considerable distance. By analyzing fauna from surrounding regions, it may be possible to determine the individual's area of origin.

Table 2. List of Attributes Commonly Associated with the Piedra Phase and Rosa Phase Traditions

Attribute	Piedra Tradition (Northern San Juan)	Rosa Tradition (Upper San Juan)
Black-on-white pottery	Lino, Chapin, or Piedra	Rosa
Redware ceramics	relatively common to rare	rare
Temper	andesite-diorite	quartz-feldspar
Paint	organic	glaze with organic binder
Surface architecture	substantial, habitation and storage	insubstantial, storage only?
Pit structures	rectangular, wingwalls, non-bifurcated vent system, abundant floor features	round, no wingwalls, bifurcated vent system, paucity of floor features
Site layout	formal, northwest-southeast orientation	informal
Settlements	often aggregated	often dispersed
Enclosures	present	present

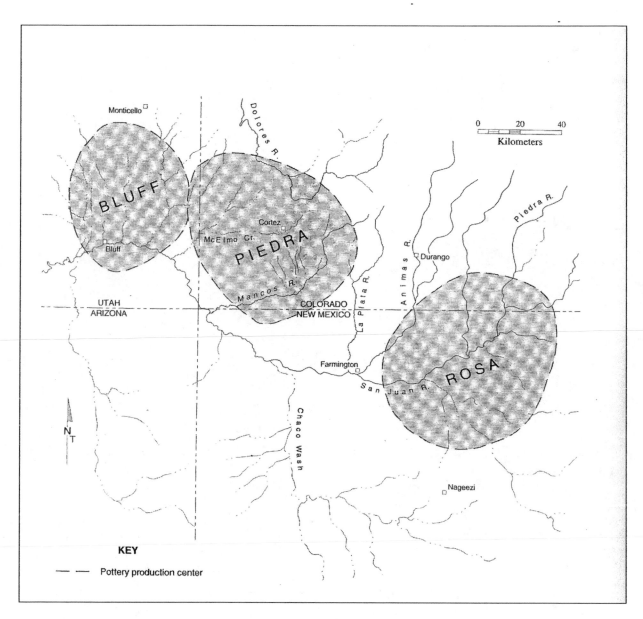

Figure 5. Map of the different ceramic production areas around Durango during the Pueblo I period (from Wilshusen 1999:208).

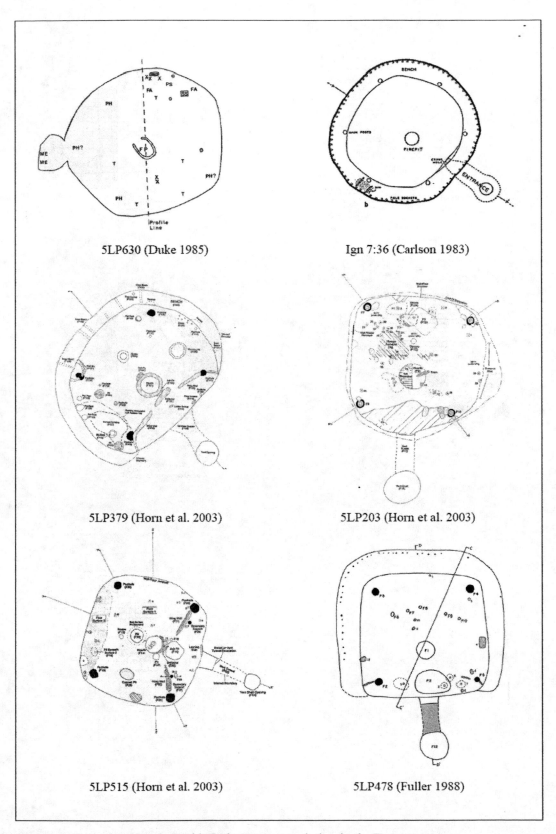

5LP630 (Duke 1985)   Ign 7:36 (Carlson 1983)

5LP379 (Horn et al. 2003)   5LP203 (Horn et al. 2003)

5LP515 (Horn et al. 2003)   5LP478 (Fuller 1988)

Figure 6. Examples of early Pueblo I pit structure variation in the Durango area.

Analysis of the presence and distribution of nonmetric skeletal traits provides complementary information relating to cultural origins through the assessment of biological distance. Primary nonmetrics under observation in this study are cranial sutural bones, proliferative ossifications (hyperostotic traits), and ossification failure (hypostotic traits) (Buikstra and Ubelaker 1994). It is accepted that such traits are inherited and often population-specific in humans and other species, and the differential distribution of such traits in individuals across habitation sites constitutes strong evidence of the existence of discrete genetic groups.

Incidence of dental opacities will also be evaluated with respect to cultural origins. Martin and Goodman (1995) found that skeletal material recovered from previous excavations in Ridges Basin exhibited high frequencies of dental opacities. These defects are not clearly related to any physiological stress or deficiency, but rather are likely caused by "high fluoride intake or an unusual pattern of intake of other trace minerals, which affected the calcification of enamel hydroxyapatite" (Martin and Goodman 1995:17). The formation of opacities is thus tied to the consumption of minerals that may be differentially present in various natural environments and/or may have a genetic component. A group of individuals with a high frequency of dental opacities may have resided in the same environment during the process of dental development. Thus, tracing the distribution of opacities across communities in Ridges Basin may provide information about the composition, movement, and relatedness of people residing in this area.

With the methods described above, we will attempt to measure genetic or isotope variation in individuals so that we can address questions of cultural diversity and origins in Ridges Basin. Certain learned cultural practices also vary across different Puebloan groups, and some of these practices leave observable signatures on the skeleton. For example, traditional sitting or squatting postures are often different across cultural groups and lead to skeletal modification of the bones of the legs and feet. Anatomically, sitting or squatting postures may involve dorsiflexion, hyperdorsiflexion, and plantar flexion of the ankle joint, relating to the nature and degree of ankle flexion from different kneeling and squatting postures. Habitual dorsiflexion of the ankle produces distinctive facets on the anterior surface of the distal tibia from pressure at the articulation with the talus (Merbs 1983). In contrast, sitting postures involving hyperdorsiflexion involve flexion of the toes as well as the ankle, putting pressure on the metatarsal-phalangeal joints (Ubelaker 1979). Such pressure can result in an expansion of the distal articular surfaces of the metatarsals involving the superior surface, "forming a flat facet that may extend into a ridge connecting the lateral tubercles" (Ubelaker 1979:74). The articular surface of the first metatarsal appears to be particularly sensitive to hyperdorsiflexion (Molleson 1994). Investigating the distribution of skeletal signatures of different sitting postures across sites and site clusters in Ridges Basin and on Blue Mesa can potentially establish the existence of discrete groups of people engaging in different learned cultural practices.

Traditional methods of transporting loads and carrying children also vary across prehistoric and historic southwestern communities. Raw materials such as clay, objects such as water jars, or other items may be transported on one's head, balanced on the hip, or carried using a tumpline stretched across the forehead. Preferred methods differ across culture groups, and each practice results in a distinctive skeletal signature. The habitual practice of carrying loads on the top of the head can lead to accelerated degenerative changes in the cervical vertebrae, and the use of a tumpline may contribute to differential development of the mastoid processes. The tendency to carry children or other heavy loads with the non-dominant arm (freeing up the dominant arm for more detailed activities) may result in asymmetrical development of muscle insertion sites or expressions of osteoarthritis. As noted above, preferences for methods of load carrying are often patterned cultural behaviors, and differences among the skeletal signatures of load carrying may signal membership in different cultural groups.

Osteological analyses of human burials in the Prehispanic Southwest indicate that cranial deformation resulting from the cultural practice of cradleboarding first occurred during the PI period (Brew 1946). Across the Southwest, different communities adopted and engaged in this practice at different rates and in different frequencies, and different methods of cradleboarding left different cranial signatures. It is possible that some cultural variation relating to this practice existed among the Ridges Basin and Blue Mesa communities. If so, different cultural groups may be extrapolated from the presence or absence of cranial deformation related to cradleboarding. The primary forms of cranial deformation in the prehistoric Southwest involved lambdoidal or occipital flattening, although frontal flattening occurred as well (Buikstra and Ubelaker 1994). Variation in cradleboarding practices represents another fertile area of investigation for documenting the presence of different prehistoric culture groups.

In general, differences in health profiles among the occupants of different habitation sites can provide information regarding differential access to nutritional resources, exposure to violence, tendency toward disease and infection, and morbidity and mortality. Along these lines, the Ridges Basin skeletal population will be studied for evidence of porotic hyperostosis, systemic infections, stature, dental pathology, osteoarthritis, and trauma.

These data can be combined with material culture evidence such as ceramics, projectile points, and architecture to draw further inferences about the distinctive features of different groups of people. Using architectural stylistic data, SWCA will explore several possible models for the cultural origins of the Ridges Basin area occupants. The first model posits that the population is mostly locally derived, with a few immigrant groups contributing to the variation in pit structure morphology over time. In the second model, the population is composed entirely of immigrants from different areas. There are, of course, many possible variations on this second model. It is possible, for instance, that the Ridges Basin population consisted primarily of Rosa-style people (from the east), who were influenced by the Piedra-style (and potentially other) people, or that they were primarily Rosa people with a few Piedra-style folks living among them. What will be of interest is how homogeneous or mixed the stylistic and biological traits of the population are within and between household clusters and how the central village (the Sacred Ridge Site) compares to these patterns.

The issue of cultural origins and interaction in the PI period in Durango is not a trivial one. The history of these groups influenced not only how they organized themselves on the landscape, but also whom they interacted with and the nature of those interactions, and ultimately where they went when they abandoned the area. All of these factors have significant ramifications for early Puebloan population and community dynamics throughout the northern Southwest and into later time periods, such as the Chacoan era. Two of the most likely possibilities for the destination of populations abandoning the Ridges Basin area are the Dolores area to the west and the Fruitlands area of northern New Mexico to the southeast. Population size in both areas appears to have risen sharply at about A.D. 850 (Fetterman and Honeycutt 2001; Wilshusen 1999:235). To research this issue, SWCA will attempt to refine the abandonment chronology of Ridges Basin and Blue Mesa, assess which cultural affiliation and interaction model best fits the project area data, and refine population estimates for donor and recipient populations.

Post–PI use of the Ridges Basin area was minimal. However, even if no later habitations are present, small numbers of sherds from later ceramics have been found in the area (Allison 1995). Assessing the nature of this later use will be an ongoing goal for SWCA as we collect more data from the project area.

PROTOHISTORIC RESEARCH DESIGN

Given the limited amount of archaeological documentation of protohistoric Ute (and possibly Navajo) use of southwestern Colorado, the initial goal of SWCA's protohistoric research on the ALP project will be to aggressively seek out all protohistoric remains that may exist within the project area. From there, we will thoroughly record, expose, and sample the sites to date them, determine their cultural affiliation, reconstruct the size and nature of the groups that used them, and estimate the length of time that each was used.

Identifying protohistoric Ute sites, and demonstrating their cultural affiliation, will be simplified if Ute pottery is found. David Hill (Hill 1988) has argued that Ute pottery was made using the paddle-and-anvil technique, which caused the clay plates to line up—as can be observed in microscopic analysis of thin-sections of Ute pottery. In contrast, Navajo pottery was produced by the coil-and-scrape method, which does not cause the clay plates to line up to the same extent. Additional documentation of this distinction using sherds from the ALP project area would be useful for future Ute and Navajo archaeological research. Simply publishing photographs of thin sections and other compositional data would be a significant contribution. Documenting which techniques were used in the production of the protohistoric ceramics from the project area would indicate which tribes were using the area and to what extent, as well as indicating the extent of trade between them.

Protohistoric sites can also be recognized by the presence of Hopi Yellow Ware sherds, and the specific type found can help date the site. Hopi Yellow Ware was rapidly changing during the Protohistoric period (Wade and McChesney 1981), and ceramicists analyzing Hopi pottery from protohistoric sites will try to distinguish Jeddito Black-on-yellow (A.D. 1325–1630), Sikyatki Polychrome (A.D. 1450–1630), San Bernardo Polychrome (A.D. 1630–1680), and Payupki Polychrome (A.D. 1680–1780). Zuni and Eastern Pueblo trade wares, which are also relatively well dated, may also occur in the Ridges Basin area.

Protohistoric sites may be identifiable, and datable, in the absence of pottery. Navajo sites in the Dinétah region of northwestern New Mexico have yielded numerous tree-ring dates (e.g., Towner 1997), and many of the dates obtained in recent years reflect an aggressive protocol developed by the Bureau of Land Management (BLM) and its permit holders working in the Dinétah. Under this protocol, researchers make a special effort to recognize collapsed and partly decomposed structures (including summer brush structures), as well as the stumps or lopped branches of trees from which structural wood or firewood was obtained. Near-vanished structures can be recognized if some branch ends are axe-trimmed, and culturally modified trees have weathered, axe-cut root/branch stumps. In some cases, bows or planks were cut out of trees, leaving a sunken rectangular scar. To the extent possible, tree-ring samples are cut from all of the branches, stumps, and trees exhibiting such marks, and the sampling locations are placed on site maps. This aggressive dating protocol leads researchers to look for cultural evidence they might otherwise walk past, increasing the likelihood that protohistoric sites will be recognized and fully documented. We propose to apply the BLM's protocol in Colorado to identify and fully document protohistoric Ute sites.

Other forms of dating may reveal the presence of a protohistoric site only after the site is selected for excavation under some other rationale. Radiocarbon dates from protohistoric sites would immediately jump out from those for a prehistoric occupation. Obsidian hydration dating is fairly imprecise, but it would certainly distinguish protohistoric lithic scatter sites from Archaic ones. These sorts of samples should also be analyzed for protohistoric sites identified by other means, to pin down their age.

If a protohistoric site is identified, our goal will be to excavate that site completely and document what we can about the subsistence activities and the size and nature of the group using the site. In particular, SWCA wishes to know more about Ute subsistence practices through time, and we will conduct comprehensive subsistence studies (including pollen, flotation, phytolith, and faunal sampling and analysis) at any protohistoric sites that are encountered. If we excavate and analyze a suspected Ute site, it will be especially important to involve Colorado Ute tribal members in this effort, as it will be their history that is being documented.

Once the protohistoric sites are identified and documented, and depending on how much information is obtained, the next step will be to understand the settlement pattern reflected in those sites. Here again, recent work in Dinétah provides a model (most of this work is associated with the Fruitland Project, which was summarized in a symposium on early Navajo lifeways at the 1999 meetings of the Society for American Archaeology). The New Mexico work has focused on identifying households (represented by individual hogans), residence groups (basically extended families, represented by clusters of hogans), "outfits" (groups of related and cooperating families, represented by clusters of hogan clusters), and communities (clusters of clusters of hogan clusters, usually centered around a pueblito). Moreover, this research has shown that not all communities were contemporaneous and has begun to trace population movements from early communities to later ones. The Ute results will be different, of course, but similar analyses can be conducted to trace the composition and distribution of Ute settlement over time-space.

To examine Ute interaction with other groups, SWCA will analyze the numbers, types, and dates of trade wares found at Ute sites. We expect Hopi, Zuni, Eastern Pueblo, and Navajo ceramics, but do not know which types or in what frequencies. Also, using the same approach proposed for Archaic sites (see Prehistoric Research Design, Issue 1.3), SWCA proposes to document the frequency of imported lithic raw materials from known sources and the frequency of non-local lithic raw materials generally. If substantial trade in pottery and tool stone can be documented, it then becomes necessary to identify the products that Utes may have been trading in exchange for these goods. (While there are Spanish documents on historic trade patterns in the Four Corners area, those documents may not reflect the full range of the historic trade, and certainly do not tell us anything about trade before the Spanish arrived and altered the inter-regional economy.)

An issue of particular interest is the documentation, commemoration, and interpretation of the Ute Trail (5LP4213) through Ridges Basin. The Colorado State Historic Preservation Officer (SHPO) has determined the trail eligible for the National Register of Historic Places (NRHP) under Criteria A, B, and D. NAU and SWCA (1996) recommended mapping the trail between Towaoc and Ignacio, documenting the history of the trail and its significance to the Ute people of Colorado through oral history, and erecting a commemorative plaque above the high-water line of the reservoir. The trail route is also a logical place to look for protohistoric sites. SWCA ethnographers could document the oral histories and design the commemorative plaque, in consultation with the Colorado Ute Tribes. SWCA will also develop a Consulting Tribes Plan as part of the ALP project and submit that document as a deliverable.

HISTORIC RESEARCH DESIGN

General regional issues and patterns for the Historic period are the context for research at ALP project historic sites. Thus, in addressing the historical archaeology of the project area, we begin by discussing the regional issues and then focus on the project area itself.

History of Southwestern Colorado

The history of southwestern Colorado parallels the history of much of the Southwest and Mountain West. Historical overviews of southwestern Colorado can be found in O'Rourke (1980), Stein and Ballagh (1995), and Winter et al. (1986) (see also Buckles and Buckles 1984). The earliest documentary accounts of the region date to the time of Spanish exploration. From 1761 to 1765, Juan María de Rivera led three expeditions into the area (Leiby 1984), followed by the Dominguez and Escalante expedition of 1776 (Vélez de Escalante 1995). New Mexico Hispanics subsequently established a trail through the region for their trade with California; in the early 1800s, fur traders also began using the route, and it was they who dubbed it the Old Spanish Trail. In Ridges Basin, the Dominguez-Escalante expedition and Old Spanish Trail follows the Old Ute Trail (5LP4213). In the late 1860s, prospectors began to locate mining claims in the San Juan Mountains, and the U.S. military and mining interests restricted the indigenous Ute population to reservations. Farmers and ranchers moved in to supply the military and the miners, towns were established, and transportation and commercial systems developed to transport raw materials to markets on the East Coast and to bring in manufactured goods. The integration of the region into a national network of railroads, combined with an enormous demand for mining timbers, allowed the logging industry to develop. This period of economic development and integration was economically and socially dynamic, as farmers, ranchers, miners, railroaders, loggers, merchants, and others established enterprises, exhausted resources, and adjusted to changing market conditions.

Historical Archaeology in Southwestern Colorado

To date, historical archaeologists working in southwestern Colorado have found no direct evidence (such as artifacts or campsites) of Spanish exploration, though the general route and a number of landmarks of the Old Spanish Trail are known. In the 1980s, Steven Baker of Centuries Research began a project to document the Ute occupation of the Uncompahgre River valley (Baker 1983a–1996), attempting to find archaeological evidence of Fort Robidoux (or Fort Uncompahgre), a fur-trading outpost dating circa 1826–1836. Baker conducted research at Fort Crawford near Montrose, identifying the Los Pinos Agency at Colonia (1876–1881), and excavated at Chief Ouray's adobe home in Ouray (1876–1881) and the two adobe homes at his nearby ranch. The bulk of historical archaeology in southwestern Colorado, though, has focused on the American period, when the U.S. colonized the area. The three major historic projects conducted in the region to date are the Dolores Archaeological Project (DAP), the Dallas Creek Project, and the ALP project.

The DAP focused on archival research and oral history rather than historical archaeology (Baker 1983b:37; Duranceau 1983). Kendrick's (1982) edited volume consists of four studies that show how different historic uses of the lower Dolores River valley were reflected architecturally: Smith (1982) provided a general historical overview, Dishman (1982) summarized the farming and ranching sites, Gerhold (1982) discussed the Montezuma Valley Irrigation System, and Mausolf (1982) described the lumber company town of McPhee. Each of these studies summarized the history of a particular use of the valley, and included maps, building plans, drawings of building elevations, and photographs that were compiled during the Historic American Building Survey (HABS) documentation of the sites.

The Dallas Creek Project (Buckles 1986) dealt with the community of Dallas in a high mountain valley along the creek of the same name. Most of the valley was Ute Reservation from 1860 to 1881. Dallas was established in 1879, when gold was discovered, and the Utes were subsequently removed. Placer mining and farms constituted the initial Euroamerican uses of the valley; later uses included transportation, merchandising, logging, and coal mining. After about 1890, Dallas served primarily as a farming area supplying food to Ouray and Montrose. After World War I, the local population declined as southwestern Colorado became more connected to national and international commercial networks. The Dallas Creek Project integrated historical archaeology, history, and oral history, and included detailed mapping of sites and recording of architecture. The report contains tabular data on types and numbers of artifacts recovered from different sites and contexts.

In 1976, Centuries Research excavated the Corner Saloon in Lake Valley (the saloon burned in 1913) (Baker 1983b). During construction of skiing facilities in Telluride, Alan Reed (then of Nickens and Associates) recovered an assemblage of 1880–1920 historical artifacts that were analyzed by Jonathan Horn (also then of Nickens and Associates) and provided information on town life in Telluride during this early period (Baker

1988; Reed and Horn 1985). During the stabilization at Animas Forks, Colorado (Site 5SA153), a considerable number of artifacts was collected and analyzed during soil removal, but they were mixed assemblages from the 1880s on and are probably not particularly good comparative collections (Horn 1999). Unfortunately, little historical archaeology has been conducted in Durango (Duke and Matlock 1999:53–56), but an excavation in the downtown area uncovered the remains of a lumber mill, a hardware store, a flour mill, a slaughterhouse, and a sewer system. Limited excavations were conducted at the old Durango jail, the old city dump has been documented, and archaeologists have apparently recorded a number of historic features exposed during construction, including a wine cellar behind the Strater Hotel, a brewery or bottling company at the corner of 14th and Main, foundations, privies, streets, the original oak-stave water line, and hitching rings (Duke and Matlock 1999:54–56).

At Site 5LP1252, along the Animas City–Silverton Toll Road just north of Durango, Horn excavated a historic cabin, possibly a toll station, that returned a tree-ring date of 1876 (Horn et al. 1984, 1986). At Site 5LP357, along Rico Wagon Road near Durango, Horn tested two 1900–1910 structures thought to have been used by hay harvesters (Baker 1988; Horn 1986). Horn also analyzed artifacts from two twentieth-century sites, 5MT10969 and 5MV3966, near and within Mesa Verde National Park, that were impacted by a water-line installation project (Horn 1994). In the 1980s, archaeologists from the National Park Service's Midwest Archeological Center conducted excavations at Marion, Colorado, an 1889 railroad construction camp in Curecanti National Recreation Area near Gunnison (Baker 1983b:37; Rosillon 1984). Recently, for the Rocky Mountain Expansion Loop Pipeline, which follows the MAPCO pipeline through northwestern New Mexico and southwestern Colorado, Alpine Archaeological Consultants excavated several historic sites (Horn 2002, in press). Three were railroad related—an 1890 construction camp for the Rio Grande Southern Railroad (5LP1915), a circa 1892–1919 Rio Grande Southern section house known as The Hook (5LP1921), and a circa 1890s–1920s maintenance siding at Kane/Dix (5LP1920), all between Mancos and Hesperus. Site 5DL318 was a 1910s homestead just north of Dove Creek. Farther north, but as part of the same project, Alpine excavated a large portion of Carbonero (5GF1562), a coal mining community that served the Uintah Railway north of Grand Junction. Numerous archaeological surveys in the region have identified a wide range of historic sites as well. Thus, historical archaeology is accumulating data from a wide range of historic sites in southwestern Colorado that can be compared to provide a picture of everyday life for Utes, farmers, miners, railroad construction workers, coal miners, and town dwellers from about 1860 to 1940.

Historical Archaeology as Social History

Given the amount of available data, it is possible to examine changes over time in the social history of southwestern Colorado. To what extent do the histories of the various high mountain valleys of Colorado (and others in the American West) replicate each other—and to what extent are they unique? What are the causes of the similarity or uniqueness? Dishman (1982) assessed each historical period at Dolores in terms of legislation (which changed from period to period but which would have applied to all of the high mountain valleys of Colorado), minerals and crops produced, organization of production of those minerals and crops, and the commercial networks that would have governed the markets for these products. For the ALP project historical research, SWCA recommends documenting the occupation in terms of comparable categories.

In approaching the subject, however, it is important to have a sense of what can and cannot be expected from historical archaeological data. We believe that the ALP data can add to our understanding of the region's history in two ways: first, by identifying case studies for historical research, and second, by providing information not found in archives and documents. Archaeological studies commonly identify sites and settlement systems that are not discussed in published local or regional histories. In attempting to document, assess, and interpret these sites, historical archaeologists typically compile documentary and archival data, oral histories, and archaeological data that transfer sites and settlement systems into the realm of coherent written history. The DAP historical research, the Dallas Creek Project, and ALP project are examples of these types of studies. Reasons for lack of existing documentation vary. Some sites were too early to be mentioned or discussed in detail;

others were created by people who failed to attract the attention of traditional historians, or whose documentary traces are distorted by biases. In southwestern Colorado, for example, Spanish explorer-traders and later Euroamerican fur traders left little documentary evidence of their travels, and discovery of archaeological sites associated with those groups would greatly enhance our understanding of their history. Groups who were often ignored by traditional historians or whose history has suffered from biased reporting include women, laborers, and minorities (in the Southwest and Mountain West, mostly Native Americans, Mexicans, and Hispanics, but also Blacks, Chinese, Irish, and southern and eastern Europeans).

More recent social historians (Limerick et al. 1991; Olin 1986; White 1991) have focused on these groups, and historical archaeology can assist in compiling this social history by providing information on daily life. By examining the archaeological traces of specific households, historical archaeologists have been able to ascertain the ethnicity, class, gender, occupation, and ideology of the occupants of such sites. When basic facts are available in census records or similar documents, the archaeologists can provide a wealth of detail about the quality of homes, domestic activities, and the goods being consumed by families of a known social sub-group. Such information has allowed historical archaeologists to reconstruct a much broader picture of the development of the American West than was available from traditional history, as Fuller (1989) noted in his research design for the ALP project. We have identified the following historical research issues for this project.

Site Formation Processes

Before archaeologists can answer questions about such topics as subsistence, social organization, and ethnicity, they need to understand historic trash disposal patterns. For prehistoric Southwestern occupations, it is generally safe to assume that the discard products from an occupation were disposed of on-site—but for historic occupations this may or may not be the case. If all trash was disposed of on-site, it is possible to obtain a fairly complete picture of domestic consumption and thus of the lifeways reflected in that consumption. If trash was burned on site (as indicated by, for example, melted glass), archaeological interpretations must allow for a partial elimination of the archaeological record. If trash was hauled off, it is even more difficult to reconstruct lifeways based on discard patterns. Based on SWCA's 1995 reconnaissance, it appears that during the late 1800s and early 1900s, most trash at historic sites in the project area was dumped on-site. At two sites (5LP445 [not eligible] and 5LP579), trash from the mid to late 1900s was probably hauled away.

Subsistence

The goal of reconstructing subsistence is not so much to try to figure out what the site occupants ate (in general terms, we know this already) as it is to reconstruct their subsistence strategies. Presumably, the residents of Porter, a coal-mining town, were purchasing more food than the residents of the farms and ranches in Ridges Basin. If, however, the ranching sites were mostly line camps, the laborers at those camps might have consumed mostly purchased food instead of producing their own. On the Navajo Indian Irrigation Project, Gilpin (1993) found that some Navajos were essentially subsistence herders, that is, they lived primarily on the products of herding and purchased few foodstuffs, mostly staples such as flour, lard, coffee, and baking powder. Other Navajos, however, and all of the Euroamerican ranchers in the project area, were commercial herders, trading their livestock for canned goods and other commercially produced foods.

Demography

Historic sites in the American West housed a wide variety of social groups, often most evident in gender ratios and the presence or absence of children. At the Carlota Mine area in Arizona (Ballagh and Goodman 1999), for example, most sites were occupied by a male work force and a few women. During construction of Roosevelt Dam (Bassett 1994), also in Arizona, most of the camps were occupied by unaccompanied Euroamerican males, while Apache construction workers brought their entire families. Based on problems experienced with the Euroamerican work force at Roosevelt, the U.S. Reclamation Service established a more family oriented camp at Elephant Butte Dam that included an ice cream parlor and a moving-picture hall and prohibited alcohol (Phillips 1996). It will be instructive to examine the demographics of the town of Porter and the ranch habitations

in Ridges Basin (Miller 1992; History Committee of the Fort Lewis Mesa Reunion 1994). At Porter (and adjacent sites), for example, it would be useful to know if households consisted primarily of men, or if family groups were present. It would be useful to know if the ranching sites in Ridges Basin were primarily line camps occupied by men, or family farms and ranches. Once the demographic composition of a community has been established, we will be able to ask why the community developed as it did—specifically, why some communities were demographically complete but others were not.

Ethnicity

At the historic component of Site NP-1 in northeastern New Mexico (Gilpin 1987), documentary evidence and architecture (most notably a corner fireplace and a bread oven or *horno*) suggested a Hispanic family, but the trash (including transfer-printed china, pressed glass, jewelry, and fancy buttons) indicated that the residents had adopted Victorian values in dining, sex and gender roles, and so forth. In southeastern Colorado, Church (2000) has shown that ethnicity among families was not clear-cut, as many family groups consisted of a Euroamerican male and his Hispanic or Indian wife, or a Hispanic male and his Euromaerican or Indian wife. In some cases, the archaeological record provides clear clues to ethnicity; more often, documentary records indicate ethnicity but are largely silent on its behavioral implications (census records are a good example). When ethnicity is known from documents, archaeological assemblages associated with different ethnic groups (or specific mixes of groups) can be compared to see whether ethnic affiliation affected patterns of subsistence and consumption.

Ideology and World View

The Industrial Revolution was a time of change that affected every aspect of society. In response, the associated Victorian style emphasized highly structured organization and strong distinctions in race, ethnicity, class, gender, work, home life, and public appearance, as communicated by architecture, furnishings, tableware, and clothing. Baker (1983c) and others have argued that the industrialization of the American West and the concomitant local adoption of Victorian style provide an important research focus for historical archaeology in the region.

One of the manifestations of the Victorian worldview was an intensification of the earlier Georgian emphasis on "rational" organization of space. Some sites in the ALP project area have neatly aligned buildings, in keeping with Victorian style; at others, however, buildings are strung out along natural topographic features such as ridges and streams. Porter is not a typical company town designed by engineers and laid out in grids, perhaps because of the size of the company that designed it or the scale of the operation, or because the community was set up by the workers themselves, not company engineers. At least two of the ranches (5LP192 and 5LP579) are formal in plan; at least two others (5LP190 in Ridges Basin and 5LP518 [possibly mining related] in Wildcat Canyon) are not. SWCA's archaeologists will look at architecture and artifact assemblages (especially furnishings, clothing, and tableware) to see to what extent and in what ways people living at these different types of sites had adopted Victorian style—and, by extension, the Victorian world view.

Historical Archaeology in the Project Area

Previous Research

Overviews of the history of the project area can be found in Baugh (1989), Stein and Ballagh (1995), and Winter et al. (1986). Baugh focuses on coal mining in Wildcat Canyon. The other two sources provide histories of the project area as a whole. Some key events in the history of the project area are listed here:

1880	Two Cross Ranch, headquartered in Farmington, New Mexico, had a summer headquarters in Ridges Basin.
1886	Porter Coal Mine (1886–1908) established.
1887	Earliest GLO map of Ridges Basin shows houses of G. N. Thompson (Two Cross Ranch), S. Nichols, S. Pruden (or Prudden), and W.C. Kibbs (or Hibbs).
1890	Rio Grande Southern Railroad line constructed up Wildcat Canyon to Porter.
1890s	Nine families in Ridges Basin.
1900–1920	Seven more farms in Ridges Basin.
1908	Porter Coal Mine closed.
1910	Porter still occupied but declining.
1909–1911	Most settlers in Ridges Basin sold farms to Dyer O. Clark, who transferred his holdings to the Durango Land Company.
1910–1930	Gates Mine in Ridges Basin.
1927	Durango Land Company sold Ridges Basin property to Porter Fuel Company.
1941	Porter Fuel Company sold its property in Ridges Basin to the Harper, Bodo, and Kikel families (the Harper and Kikel families had been in the valley since the 1900–1920 period; the Bodo Ranch property was investigated by Fort Lewis College).
1951	Rio Grande Southern Railroad operations suspended.

Surveys of the Ridges Basin project area have identified 38 historic sites. Baugh's (1989) history documented coal mining in the project area. Stein (Stein and Ballagh 1995) re-evaluated the National Register eligibility of the sites in the project area, examining their archaeological potential and conducting archival research on their historical context, and recommended that nine sites be determined eligible for the NRHP and that six sites be further investigated to determine eligibility. Stein also identified three types of historical sites: the coal-mining sites of Wildcat Canyon, the railroad and railroad-associated sites in Wildcat Canyon, and the ranching sites of Ridges Basin.

Research Concerns

Coal Mining

The primary goal of research at coal mining sites in Wildcat Canyon will be to look at each of the buildings at Porter (Site 5LP517) and the outlying sites (especially Site 5LP518) and ascertain, from architecture and artifacts, the function of each building (whether dwelling or commercial) and the ethnicity, class, demographics, and worldview of the households represented at dwellings. Once these social attributes have been defined, we can examine the reasons for differences within the study area (for example, how coal-mining camps were different from other types of settlements) and between the study area and other parts of southwestern Colorado.

Railroading

Railroading is represented at two sites in Wildcat Canyon: 5LP519 (a railroad grade) and 5LP528 (a stone structure). At Site 5LP519, Stein (Stein and Ballagh 1995:69) recommended more detailed recording of the techniques and materials used to construct different segments of the grade. At Site 5LP528, the architecture and artifacts need to be more thoroughly investigated to ascertain the function of the site and extract information on ethnicity, class, gender, and worldview. If these data are collected, this site can be included in the analysis of inter-site social variability.

Ranching

Most ranching sites in the project area are in Ridges Basin, but a few are in Wildcat Canyon. Historical archaeological studies of ranching will focus on both the ranching landscape in Ridges Basin and individual ranches.

How did the ranching landscape of Ridges Basin form, and what did it look like? At one time the Mountain West was dominated by a continuous ranching landscape, but today much of that landscape is disappearing. We have a fair amount of archival data on the subject— maps, property records, tax records, and so on. Using such records as a baseline, it will be possible to record the ranching landscape that remains. The effort will include both historical archaeological studies at sites, and photographing and otherwise documenting historical attributes of the general landscape. As Stein (Stein and Ballagh 1995:24) commented, "Relatively little is known about specific agricultural improvements made by the aforementioned settlers or the agricultural goods produced by them." One way to learn about early agricultural improvements would be to map the irrigation system. When SWCA re-evaluated the historic sites in the project area in the fall of 1994, we noticed that few irrigation features had been recorded as sites. Also, most archaeologists simply ignore fence lines (and the rea-

sons behind their placement) during survey. Historic landscapes are becoming an important issue in cultural resource management, but so far the tools for mitigating the loss are poorly developed. SWCA's documentation of the ranching landscape in the ALP study area may be a useful case study in the development of effective landscape mitigation efforts.

In studying individual ranches, SWCA will investigate the architecture and artifacts of each of the buildings at each eligible ranching site to ascertain the function of each building (dwelling, barn, storage, etc.) and gather social data on the members of the households represented. The social data can be compared to those from the mining-related sites (and possibly Site 5LP528) to examine variation across functional types. The combined ALP data can then be used to examine social variation across southwestern Colorado.

Proposed Fieldwork in the Project Area

Much of Wildcat Canyon will be outside the direct impact zone, and since the history of coal mining in this area has been covered by Baugh (1989), SWCA's major concern should probably be site preservation and management. The physical evidence of the ranching settlement system in Ridges Basin will be heavily impacted by construction of the reservoir. SWCA therefore proposes archival and historical research on the settlement system, remote sensing and ground recording of the irrigation system, and archaeological research to include instrument mapping of sites, photography and measured drawings of standing buildings and structures (to HABS/HAER [Historic American Engineering Record] standards), surface collections, and excavation of selected features.

Though most of the regional archival sources have been investigated by Baugh (1989), Stein (Stein and Ballagh 1995), and Winter et al. (1986), additional work on these resources might yield new information. Newspapers constitute perhaps the most significant untapped archival resource in the regional archives. Poring through newspapers for information is an inefficient process, but many libraries and museums have indexes of local newspapers, and if such indexes exist in southwestern Colorado or northwestern New Mexico museums or libraries, they will be used to locate newspaper references to Ridges Basin, Porter, and the various families known to have lived in the area (as discussed in Stein and Ballagh [1995]). Stein also recommends doing research in the Homestead Case Files in the National Archives. Because homesteaders were required to document improvements to a claim, the case files often contain details about homes, outbuildings, and other features.

Only a limited number of oral histories have been collected on the Euroamerican occupation of the project area. SWCA will attempt to interview individuals who lived at the historic sites included in the project, or their descendants, to learn about lifeways in coal-mining settlements and on ranches.

Existing archaeological documentation of the nine eligible sites and six potentially eligible sites consists of sketch maps, photographs of arbitrarily selected views of sites, features, and buildings, and arbitrary samples of artifacts. SWCA proposes seven tasks: (1) additional work in regional archival sources to fill in gaps in our understanding of the history of the project area, particularly in response to new information from and questions raised by oral history and archaeological research; (2) research in the homestead files, as recommended by Stein; (3) conducting oral history; (4) recording of sites and architectural features, including instrument mapping of sites, recording of standing buildings and structures to HABS/HAER standards, and narrative descriptions of the buildings, structures, and archaeological remains; (5) collection of surface artifacts (either 100 percent or samples from defined bounded spaces within the site); (6) excavation of features; and (7) limited testing to see whether additional features are present (for example, looking for privies at sites with standing architecture). We recommend carrying out Tasks 1–5 at all eligible and potentially eligible historic sites, with the goal of collecting comparable data from all sites in the project area and providing information for management of sites that will not be destroyed by construction or impoundment. Excavation (Tasks 6 and 7) will be restricted to sites and features within construction zones and impoundment areas.

ANALYTICAL METHODS

Analytical methods for an archaeological project of such magnitude will necessarily be complex. The following discussion outlines only the basic methods we will use for the project and how they will relate to our research design. More specific and detailed methods will be documented in analytical manuals to be prepared for specific aspects of the project and will include a ceramics manual, a lithic artifacts manual, a database manual, and so forth. These manuals will be considered deliverables to be submitted to the client for review and will be available to researchers interested in the final datasets.

Geographic Information System

SWCA will integrate a GIS at the very heart of the ALP research efforts. A GIS automatically provides spatially referenced data that can then be examined through simple but very powerful inductive explorations, or through mathematical and Boolean methods. The research objectives of this project involve time as well as space, but time values can easily be added to a GIS. Thus, GIS becomes a way to ease the analysis, interpretation, and communication of both synchronic and diachronic social patterns.

GIS data take the form of themes, which include spatial entities with variables and attributes. Many thematic datasets directly relevant to this project already exist and can be obtained from agencies and commercial sources. Others must be compiled from data gathered during this project or previous studies. The various themes can then be linked through spatial reference, allowing for the cross-correlation of geographical and archaeological datasets. By building GIS-ready spatial and other references into all project databases, SWCA will ensure that archaeological data can be downloaded directly into GIS. Table 3 provides a sample of the data sets or themes required to address the specific issues in our research proposal.

Table 3. Selected GIS Data Sets Relevant to the ALP Project

Problem Domain	Research Issue	Acquired Data Themes	Generated Data Themes
The Hunting and Gathering Lifeway	Archaic Site Structure and Settlement	Faunal taxa seasonal range	Archaeological sites by type and period
		Vegetation cover	
		Surface hydrology	Intrasite complexity (features and loci)
	Archaic Subsistence	Soils	
		Digital elevation models (DEM)	
	Mobility and Interregional Relationships	Regional geology	Lithic source locations
			Interregional distribution of archaeological sites by time and affiliation
			Interregional distribution of projectile point styles
The Transition to Agriculture	Basketmaker II Site Structure and Settlement	Surface hydrology	Floodplain model
		DEM	
	Cultural Origins, Interregional Relationships, and Abandonment	DEM	Lithic source locations
		Climate model	
The Early Puebloan Occupation	The Pueblo I Household		Distribution of sites over time
			Intrasite composition
			Ceramic production centers
			Clay sources
			Ceramic temper sources
	The Household Cluster and the Community	STATSGO/SSURGO	Intrasite organization
		DEM	Intersite organizational variability
		Faunal taxa distributions	Clay sources
		Vegetation cover	Temper sources
			Intersite variation of game element distribution
	Comparing Ridges Basin and Blue Mesa	Biodiversity	Population density
		STATSGO/SSURGO	
	Cultural Origins, Interregional Relationships, and Abandonment of the Area		Site distributions by period
			Intrasite complexity by time
			Trait distribution

The ALP project GIS will serve to actualize specific research activities called for in the research design and to promote the visualization of spatial and temporal relationships of data from a broad spectrum of thematic entities. GIS is also an effective way to explore data and develop new intuitive observations and insights that will stimulate objective analyses not yet conceived by the project.

SWCA will use a variety of GIS and imaging software platforms to facilitate the research objectives of the ALP project, including ArcView, IDRISI, and ERDAS Imagine. The final products will be translated into formats compatible with agency systems to facilitate future use of the data. It will also be possible to create read-only GIS products (online or on CD-ROM) to help bring project results to life—for professionals and the general public alike.

Analyses

Ceramic Analysis

The ceramic analysis will support the broader research goals of the project by documenting aspects of ceramic variability and abundance relevant to chronology, occupation span, and the kinds of activities that occurred at sites. Typological identification of sherds will be the primary means of summarizing ceramic assemblage variation. Quantification of typological data will be useful for ceramic dating and estimating ceramic discard. Analysis of rim sherd and whole vessel morphology will allow inferences about the functions of ceramic vessels and the activities for which they were used. Oxidation studies, clay and temper resource surveys, and thin-section analyses will address questions about ceramic production and exchange. Finally, design attribute studies will characterize ceramic styles and allow comparisons of style use among different sites, both within the project area and between the project area and areas nearby. Style use should reflect interaction in the form of either learning contexts or active uses of style. The ceramic analysis will be conducted at SWCA's analytical laboratory under the direct supervision of the Ceramic Analysis Director, James R. Allison (Appendix B).

Typology

All recovered ceramics will be classified according to a modified version of the traditional Mesa Verde and Upper San Juan ceramic classification systems, consistent with previous studies of Ridges Basin pottery (Allison 1995). Ridges Basin is near the boundary between the Mesa Verde and Upper San Juan culture regions, and a minority of sherds in the archaeological assemblages can be unambiguously classified in one system or the other (Breternitz et al. 1974; Wilson and Blinman 1993, 1995b). Many other sherds, such as grayware body sherds, lack attributes that would allow them to be classified to a specific type in either system. Still others would be given a different name depending on which system was used—for example, a plain gray rim with crushed igneous rock temper could be called Chapin Gray in the Mesa Verde region and Arboles Gray in the Upper San Juan.

The modified system avoids potential problems arising from these ambiguities by using a flexible classification based on ware, temper, paint type, and style of decoration. Specific type names are assigned only when they are unambiguous. Temper will be identified with a binocular microscope, but only on a sample of the recovered pot sherds, which will further limit the number of sherds that can be assigned to specific types. Following Wilson and Blinman (1993, 1995a), informal or grouped types will be used where appropriate, and the classification will be explicitly sherd-based. Each sherd will be classified according to the characteristics it exhibits, even if sherds from the same vessel might be assigned to different formal or informal types.

Several other variables to be recorded during the basic typological analysis are useful mainly for the information they provide about ceramic production or the functions of ceramic artifacts. These variables include vessel form, the part of the vessel form represented, surface treatment, firing mistakes or post-firing modifications, and presence of surface deposits such as soot, organic residue, or fugitive pigments.

Vessel Morphology

Several morphological attributes of rim sherds will be documented. Specifically, orifice diameters will be estimated by comparing rim curvature to a chart of circles of various diameters. Orifice diameter suggests vessel function because it is related to ease of accessing contents. Also, jar orifices appear to correlate strongly with vessel size. Where rims can be oriented, as much of the vessel profile as possible will be drawn. With whole or reconstructed vessels, vessel volumes will be estimated from drawings of vessel profiles or measured directly from the amount of sand necessary to fill the vessel.

Oxidation Studies

Refiring pot sherds to fully oxidize them eliminates variation in sherd color caused by differences in vessel use, post-depositional processes, and the original firing of the vessel. The relationship between refired colors and clay sources used may be complex, however. Sherds that oxidize to similar colors may have been made with clays from different sources that have similar amounts of iron (which is the most important factor in oxidized color). In such cases, the clays may be from the same geologic formation and may have been created by similar processes—but clays from different formations may contain similar amounts of iron. The relationship is further complicated by the fact that potters sometimes mix different clays; refired colors may therefore reflect the specific mixture or clay recipe rather than a single geologic source. Still, if a sample of pottery refires to a variety of colors, as sherds from Ridges Basin do (Allison 1995), multiple distinct clay sources and/or recipes must have been used.

Oxidation studies of recovered sherds will involve removing small nips from the sherds and refiring them in an electric kiln, which will be heated to 950EC (1,740EF) for one hour. After cooling to room temperature, the nips will be removed, and the oxidized color of each sample will be matched to the closest tile on a Munsell color chart. For most analyses of the data, the refired Munsell colors will be aggregated into groups based on color groups used in previous oxidation studies (Allison 2000; Mills et al. 1993; Windes 1977).

Oxidation studies are an imprecise way of characterizing clay variability, but they have the advantage of being inexpensive, which allows for study of large samples. Sampling for oxidation studies will focus on rim sherds and other (mostly decorated) sherds that are obviously from vessels not represented by rims. Where ceramic assemblages can be associated with households, this sampling strategy will be used to approximate the composition of the total vessel assemblage used over the life of the household.

Oxidation studies of sherds will be complemented by clay and temper resource studies. These will involve collecting clays and potential tempering materials from Ridges Basin and surrounding areas, while carefully documenting the location and geologic setting of the collected materials. The clays will be characterized in terms of their plasticity and shrinkage, and tiles from clays suitable for ceramic production will be fired in an electric kiln under the same conditions used for the sherd oxidation studies. Potential tempering materials will be examined under a binocular microscope, and a sample of the specimens most similar to materials actually found in pottery will be thin-sectioned, along with a small sample of the pottery.

Design Attribute Studies

Whole vessels, rim sherds, and large painted sherds will undergo design attribute analysis, which will include recording details of vessel morphology (such as rim shape) that appear to be stylistic, as well as attributes of painted designs. The analysis of painted designs will record line widths and design elements on all painted sherds included in this analysis. Design layout and symmetry will also be recorded on whole vessels and on sherds that are large enough to exhibit the structure of the design.

Stone Artifact Analysis

The lithic artifact analytical structure proposed by SWCA employs three distinct levels in an interactive analysis system. This three-level approach will allow maximum efficiency in data recording, storage, and manipulation, while maintaining the flexibility to apply specific data to given research or project management issues as well as the ability to apply all possible data in more robust analytical situations.

The first analytical level, to be conducted at the field-processing laboratory, will be designed to provide a quick inventory for basic description of materials as context groupings (sites or major parts thereof), to inform further excavation or analysis, and to provide coarse-grained inter- and intra-context comparisons. As field-bagged materials are washed, counted, catalogued, and sorted, lithic materials in each context will be separated into general and easily recognizable groupings. Flaked stone items will be grouped only as projectile points, other modified tools, cores, flakes, and shattered materials. Ground stone items will be grouped as manos, metates, ornaments, haftable items, and all others. This approach will make preliminary data available quickly and with little additional effort on the part of the processing laboratory staff. The data may also be used to facilitate comparison with, and inclusion of, previously assembled ALP materials or analytical data.

A second level of stone tool analysis will be a more detailed examination of each item, or of a sample of items from provenience contexts with large and redundant assemblages. The results of this analysis will form the core of the lithic analytical dataset for addressing issues raised by the research design. This analysis level will include both flaked and ground tools, and will record variables/values for raw materials, production technology, types, metrics, and function. The analysis will be performed at SWCA's analytical laboratory under the direct supervision of the Lithic Analysis Director, Carl Phagan.

Each item will be given a unique identifying designation as a case in the appropriate data file. The basic flaked stone analysis system will include the provenience variables that link all project data files, two or three raw material variables, two or three size variables, weight, item completeness, several key production technological variables, two or three functional variables, and one or more typological assignments, thus producing both interval- and ordinal-level data. Variables in the ground stone analysis system will be similar in character. Particular care will be taken to define analytical variables as mutually exclusive categories with mutually exclusive values. Analytical measurements and decisions will be ordered so that a trained analyst will spend no more than two minutes per item.

The third level of analytical intensity will consist of specialized analysis procedures that will be employed only in limited circumstances, for carefully controlled data groupings or contexts, in response to specific research design issues and topics. Research specialists will perform or direct such analyses; examples of potentially relevant studies include microscopic use wear analysis, organic residue analysis, refitting or conjoinables analysis, obsidian X-ray fluorescence and/or neutron activation source analysis, detailed production technology analysis of flakes, local raw materials source variability identification, and subjective and statistical taxonomic studies (particularly of projectile points). Such specialized analyses can be very informative if contextual parameters are carefully controlled, and if the behavioral implications of the resulting data are convincingly established (Phagan and Gross 1986; Phagan and Wilshusen 1988). They can also be expensive and time consuming, and their use will be carefully controlled so that detailed data are not collected except as needed to answer a specific research question.

Faunal Analysis Methods

Faunal analysis methods will support the research goals of the project by documenting aspects of faunal patterning that reflect subsistence change, functional differences in activity areas, and differences in resource access among households and communities. Taxonomic and animal portion abundances will be the basic data used to address these issues. Abundance and diversity indices will allow inferences about the relative importance and variety of hunted game in the diet, about hunting techniques, and about the distribution of animal resources among contemporaneous households. Bone condition studies (including studies of butchering and breakage patterns, bone burning, and preservation) and bone tool distributions will also aid in the reconstruction of ancient activity patterns and how these varied over time and space. The faunal analysis will be conducted at SWCA's analytical laboratory under the direct supervision of the Faunal Analysis Director, James M. Potter.

Basic Analyses

The data recorded for each analyzed bone specimen will include provenience (horizontal unit, vertical unit, level, feature), taxon, bone element, side (right, left, axial, indeterminate), condition (complete, portion), origin of fragmentation (pre-depositional, post-depositional, recent), portion (shaft, proximal end, distal end, indeterminate), epiphysis (proximal, distal, indeterminate), and count. Bones will also be examined for evidence of burning, weathering, rodent or carnivore gnawing, calcium carbonate buildup, and cultural modification, both incidental (e.g., cut marks) and intentional (to create tools or ornaments).

Every bone and bone fragment will be analyzed and included in the total counts. The exceptions will be loose teeth that appear to be from an associated jaw, which will be excluded from the total counts to minimize over-representation of species represented largely by jawbones. If no associated jaw is present within the provenience in question (i.e., the excavated level), however, loose teeth will be counted as individual specimens.

Specific- or generic-level identification of rodent phalanges, vertebrae, and ribs is difficult (Klein and Cruz-Uribe 1984), so such identifications will not be attempted. Family-level identifications will be made when identification to genus or species is not possible. To provide some level of identification for phalanges, ribs, and vertebrae that cannot be identified to the family level (and for very fragmented remains), the categories of small, medium, and large mammal or bird will be used. The screen-size used to recover each bag of bones will also be recorded. Some bones will be recovered using 1/8-inch mesh screen; most excavated deposits will be screened through 1/4-inch mesh.

Taxonomic Abundances

There are numerous methods for quantifying taxonomic abundances. Standardized bone counts by number of identifiable specimens (NISP) identified to the level of species are the most common way to make general comparisons among assemblages, though numerous assumptions underlie such an analysis. One of the more important assumptions is that each bone is independent of every other bone, that is, bone associations are assumed not to have been affected by formation processes. It is highly problematic, however, to equate 100 bones from a turkey burial (which probably represents one turkey) with 100 turkey bones from a midden

(which can represent up to 100 turkeys). Thus, a number of different variables must be controlled when using straight bone counts.

The other common method for quantifying taxonomic abundances in the Southwest is the minimum number of individuals (MNI). Whereas NISP is the actual number of specimens that have been identified to some taxonomic unit, MNI is the minimum number of complete individual animals necessary to account for the observed specimens. Grayson's (1984) main criticism of MNIs was the aggregation problem—as one's stratigraphic/provenience units become finer grained, the MNIs increase. The manner in which zooarchaeologists have traditionally dealt with these problems is to calculate both a minimum (MNI) and a maximum (NISP) number of individuals to quantify ordinal taxonomic values (i.e., a rank order of taxonomic abundance), fully cognizant that the actual number of individuals is somewhere between these two extremes.

One of the problems that arises with both methods of quantification is that percentages are often calculated in order to compare samples of different sizes. This approach introduces the closed sum problem, where one taxon's relative contribution to the diet is dependent on the relative frequency of other taxa because the totals must add up to 100. To address this issue, Correspondence Analysis (CA), a multivariate technique that uses straight counts rather than percentages or proportions, can be employed to explore variation among faunal assemblages using straight NISP or MNI values (Baxter 1994). This analytical method uses row and column marginals of a multivariate table in the same manner as a chi-square analysis to derive similarity coefficients among cells, circumventing the need for standardized proportions. In this way, comparisons among assemblages can be made using unstandardized NISP and/or MNI values.

Changes over time in faunal assemblages can help identify environmental changes, over-hunting in an area, the effects of new hunting technologies, changes in hunting organization, and the effects of the adoption of agriculture on faunal procurement and consumption. Variations across space can provide information on activity distributions (e.g., processing areas versus final discard areas), the occurrence of ritual and feasting activities, and differences in access to high-quality game or cuts of meat (Potter 1997). Taxonomic abundances can also indicate seasonal use of a site or portion of a site.

Bone Condition

The bone condition variable takes into account the effects of both natural and cultural processes on individual animal bones and assemblages of animal bones. Natural processes include attrition due to weathering or animal gnawing. Identifying these processes (or documenting their absence) can help in assessing formation processes in general, as well as the extent to which faunal patterning is due to cultural processes (Lyman 1994). Cultural processes include both intentional and unintentional modification of bones. Unintentional modification includes burning and bone breakage for extracting marrow; intentional modification includes bone tool manufacture and the production of bone ornaments. When assessed with respect to feature and artifact data, the distribution and abundance of each of these attributes can be useful in identifying activity areas and determining site or area function, including the identification of processing sites/areas and communal consumption (feasting) areas (Potter 2000). Intensity of processing of large game over time can also inform on over-hunting of the local environment (Potter 1995).

Archaeobotanical Methods

Archaeobotanical analyses will focus on documenting (1) the changing mix of wild plant foods before and leading up to the local adoption of maize agriculture, (2) when maize first appears in the local archaeological record, and under what environmental conditions, (3) the degree of dietary reliance on maize through time, and (4) the interplay between wild and domestic plants in the subsistence system through time.

The fourth issue in that list has received far too little attention from Southwest archaeologists. Some of the earliest domesticated plant assemblages in the northern Southwest (notably Archaic sites from Lukachukai and Salina Springs) combine maize with disturbance plants such as Cheno-ams. This mixed subsistence strategy is remarkably similar to later Ancestral Puebloan plant assemblages. It is therefore important to go beyond documenting the presence of specific plants to characterizing plant assemblages, enabling archaeologists to unravel the complex interplay of wild and domestic plant use through time.

The archaeobotanical analysis will be performed at SWCA's analytical laboratory under the direct supervision of the Archaeobotanical Analysis Director, Karen Adams. Long before then, however—at the start of the project—the project archaeologists will meet with the project archaeobotanist to discuss field strategies that will best meet the project's research goals. This discussion will include establishing a field protocol and defining standard sample sizes, loci, intervals, and methods. The proposed pre-field collaboration will ensure that the best possible samples are acquired to contribute to defined research issues (Adams 2001; Adams and Gasser 1980; Bohrer and Adams 1977). For all data types (reproductive parts and wood charcoal acquired either via flotation samples or as macrofossil samples), criteria of identification will be provided, along with standard databases of the raw data. A comprehensive framework for accumulating insights for interpretation will be incorporated at the writing stage and will include plant part condition, archaeological context, ethnographic analogy, archaeological analogy, and ecological information (Adams 2001:68). Data will be examined in terms of taxon/part ubiquity, rank order, and in other ways appropriate to the research. Archaeobotanical interns will assist with all analyses, interpretation, and write-up.

Flotation Samples

Standardized flotation samples will be measured to verify their volume, then processed by means of a water separation system (e.g., Bohrer and Adams 1977) to extract light fractions. The light fractions will be subdivided by particle size (> 4.0 mm, 2.0–4.0 mm, 1.0–2.0 mm, 0.5–1.0 mm, < 0.5 mm) for ease of microscopic examination. All available material in the largest particle size will be examined to retrieve and identify non-charcoal specimens. For the smaller particles, sub-sampling is often required to reduce redundancy in information by accounting for the maximum number of separate plant taxa/parts within each sample, rather than providing accurate counts of every single specimen preserved within it. This approach presumes that presence/absence data for samples examined provide more interpretable information about past human behavior than do the actual counts of specimens within samples. The ecological concept of the "species area curve," developed by ecologists to know when sampling can reasonably be curtailed, has been adapted to flotation samples (Adams 1993). The abundance of taxa/parts preserved within a particle size guides how much or how little effort is spent on it before moving on to the next size. Material that is < 0.5 mm in maximum dimension is generally not examined, as few seeds are that small; usually only unidentifiable seed fragments are found in this size range.

Identifications will be based on a regional collection of reproductive plant parts, backed by herbarium specimens, along with seed identification manuals (e.g., Martin and Barkley 1961). References to identification criteria will be provided (e.g., Murray and Adams 2001), or new descriptions will be written. Specialized taxa (e.g., grasses) will be described in a uniform way (Adams 2001:70).

Wood Charcoal in Flotation Samples

By convention, wood charcoal identification is based on 20 fragments per flotation sample; each fragment must be large enough to retain anatomical features. Freshly snapped cross sections often provide enough anatomical detail for reasonable taxonomic identity (Adams 2001). A collection of modern specimens representing many of the tree and shrub species of the region will provide comparative materials for the ALP charcoal analysis, as will published references (e.g., Minnis 1987). As with reproductive parts, criteria of identification for wood charcoal will be referenced or developed. Uncharred plant materials within samples will also be noted, to provide a perspective on post-depositional disturbance processes.

Macrofossil Samples

Large plant parts retrieved in the field will also be examined. Some will be described in more detail (e.g., *Zea mays* parts), and some will be sub-sampled (e.g., charcoal specimens) as described above.

Human Remains Osteological Analyses

All analysis and treatment of human remains discovered during the course of the ALP project will be in keeping with the guidelines identified in the Native American

Graves Protection and Repatriation Act Plan of Action (NAGPRA POA) outlined in Appendix 2 of the RFP. Osteological analysis will be conducted according to the guidelines outlined in *Standards for Data Collection from Human Skeletal Remains* (Buikstra and Ubelaker 1994). SWCA personnel treat human remains with dignity and respect at all times. Standard osteological analysis includes determination of age, sex, stature, affinity, dental condition, pathology, taphonomic effects, and trauma. Measurements will be taken of all cranial elements, dentition, and long bones. Non-metric trait analysis will be conducted on all cranial and dental elements recovered. Dr. Elizabeth Perry, Project Osteologist, will supervise all aspects of recovery, analysis, and reburial of the remains.

Geomorphology

The geomorphologist for the ALP project will be Dr. Kirk Anderson. Geomorphological analyses will focus on the following four primary issues: site formation processes, prehistoric agriculture, chronological interpretation, and landscape evolution and reconstruction. A geomorphological analysis of site formation processes will be investigated in detail for each site as needed and in consultation with the project geomorphologist. Prehistoric agriculture will be explored through analysis of existing soil maps and nutrient data, which may help explain such problems as the distribution of certain sites and the potential for prehistoric crop production in the region. Systematic soil investigations may augment these data.

Addressing the prehistoric research questions requires the documentation of landscape changes through time through geomorphological analysis. The actual physical landscape responds to climatic changes and human land-use. In turn, the ability of humans to live on the landscape depends on maintaining relatively constant landscape and environmental conditions. The three prehistoric periods represented in Ridges Basin reflect not only cultural differences but almost certainly environmental variation. Thus, several questions arise. How did environmental changes during the Archaic influence human-land interactions and the transition to agriculture? What geomorphological changes (e.g., soil stability) influenced the transition to agriculture or the Early Puebloan occupation? And what changes might have occurred during the Early Puebloan occupation, such as arroyo formation or soil erosion, to cause the area to be abandoned relatively early in the Puebloan sequence? By constructing a geomorphic map of the surficial deposits of Ridges Basin, and by obtaining radiocarbon age control on deposits, landforms, soils, and episodes of downcutting, we can better understand the dynamic interactions, linkages, and feedback mechanisms between humans and the landscape.

To address the problems related to landscape changes, three areas of investigation will be undertaken: (1) a geomorphic map, intimately related to archaeological site selection and temporal affiliation, will be produced from 1:6000 stereo aerial photographs; (2) landscape elements and landforms will be defined based on geomorphic position, soil development and stratigraphic correlations (through examination of backhoe trench profiles), and absolute age as determined by radiocarbon analysis for the different-aged landforms related to archaeological sites; and (3) systematic analysis of soil physical and chemical properties will be undertaken as needed to better understand the prehistoric agricultural setting.

Historical Artifact Analysis

Historical archaeologists have devoted a great deal of discussion to methods of classifying historical artifacts, and numerous classificatory schemes have been advanced. In general, most historical artifact analysts classify artifacts according to (1) material type and method of manufacture, (2) function, or (3) some hybrid of the two. SWCA will analyze each artifact according to the first two of those categories. The condition of each artifact (broken, whole, burned/melted, modified) will also be recorded. This analytical methodology was used with success on the Navajo Indian Irrigation Project (NIIP) in northwestern New Mexico (Duran and McKeown 1980; Gilpin and McKeown 1983).

Recording materials and manufacturing technology is useful for two reasons. First, these are often not as ambiguous as function, and second, they provide the most information on date of manufacture. The classification of artifacts by material and method of manufacture will follow the classification used on the NIIP (Duran and McKeown 1980; McKeown 1983). Classi-

fying historical artifacts by materials and manufacturing technology often separates artifacts that serve the same function, however. As an example, buttons can be made of bone, shell, ceramics, glass, metal, rubber, or plastic, and a report based on typologies that rely exclusively on materials and manufacturing technology will discuss this class of artifacts in separate sections. Recording function allows us to reconstruct past behavior and also allows us to compare our data with other assemblages that used the artifact pattern system of analysis pioneered by South (1977). The functional classification system will be a combination of that proposed by Sprague (1981:255-258) and a museum classification system devised by Robert G. Chenhall (1978) and revised by Blackaby and Greeno (1988). Condition is important because it tells us about site formation processes. We are most interested in such things as whether trash was burned and how many and what types of artifacts were recycled.

FIELD METHODS

The following discussion outlines the basic field methods that SWCA will employ and how they relate to our research design. More specific methods will be documented in the project field manual. Between contract award and the start of fieldwork, a draft field manual was submitted for review and comment, and a revised draft was submitted in 2004 (see Appendix C).

Excavation Methods

Horizontal and Vertical Control

SWCA will maintain horizontal control of artifacts, features, and sites through a combination of high-resolution GPS, total station mapping, and traditional Cartesian grids. The spatial data generated by these techniques will be universalized (i.e., translated into UTM eastings and northings) in databases. The SWCA team and future researchers will thus be able to easily synthesize large amounts of data from across the project area, as well as access and analyze data from specific proveniences such as features.

Vertical control during excavation will be maintained by establishing a primary datum off-site or in an area of a site that will remain undisturbed until excavations are complete. Site datums will also be tied into actual elevations (above mean sea level) using the total station or a high-resolution GPS unit. At each feature or unit excavated at a site, at least one subdatum will be placed near the work area to ensure vertical control during the excavation. The subdatum elevations will be derived from the main site datum using a total station or instrument level. Like horizontal controls, vertical controls will be universalized in the databases as well as maintained in terms of distances relative to immediate ground surface and the site datum.

Surface Collection

Surface collections will be conducted at sites to provide information on artifact distributions and associations and to identify artifact clustering prior to subsurface investigations. One particular concern is documenting differences between Archaic, Basketmaker, Puebloan, and Protohistoric surface lithic assemblages. Analysis of surface assemblages, including those from previously collected sites, will allow researchers to establish possible quantitative differences among surface assemblages from temporally and functionally distinct sites.

Surface collection will be structured and controlled by a Cartesian grid system established across the surface of the site. Because of the high potential for artifact movement from on-site erosional processes, artifacts on the modern ground surface will not be point located. If finer spatial resolution is deemed necessary to identify surface distribution patterns, a tighter grid system can be used in lieu of point proveniencing.

Remote Sensing Pilot Study

Mechanical grading/stripping is a quick, efficient method for locating pit features, but in most cases the feature is detected after the associated prehistoric surface has been removed or thoroughly disturbed. Remote sensing can help solve this problem. SWCA therefore proposes to conduct a pilot study on one or more sites with the potential to have subsurface features and explore which techniques or combination of techniques works best to locate hearths and pit features. SWCA proposes to subject a sample of Archaic and BMII sites to remote sensing (magnetometer and soil resistivity) studies to locate possible subsurface features within

sites (see Prehistoric Research Design). The goal of the pilot study will be to allow features (and the areas around features) to be hand-exposed so that they can be excavated without losing the association with use surfaces and artifacts on those surfaces. If the initial effort is successful, a larger sample of sites may be investigated using remote sensing.

Mona Charles, the Director of the Fort Lewis Archaeological Field School, has agreed to work with SWCA to meet all of our remote sensing needs. Fort Lewis College currently owns and operates three remote sensing instruments—a Geoscan FM 36 fluxgate gradiometer, a Geoscan RM15 resistance meter, and a White's LXT spectrum E series metal detector.

Mechanical Excavations

Archaeologists often use backhoes during testing and data recovery to delineate site boundaries, locate and define subsurface features, and quickly remove sterile or redundant fill from structure interiors and large horizontal areas. During any mechanical excavation on a site, an archaeologist will be present to monitor the earth removal and ensure that cultural features are not adversely affected. Backhoes will be used for two basic purposes: excavation of trenches and horizontal stripping.

Although backhoe trenching does not expose pit stains as quickly and efficiently as grader excavation, and although trenching tends to destroy a larger percentage of each feature, remains exposed in profile retain the stratigraphic and use-surface associations often lost by large-scale stripping. Given the goals of the prehistoric research design, initial trenching will generally be preferable to initial stripping. In most cases the trenches will be excavated with a 24-inch-wide toothed bucket. Placement of the trenches will be determined by the project field supervisors and site crew chiefs using both systematic and judgmental methods, but will in all cases be the minimum distance apart needed to identify any stratigraphic relationships that may be present, generally no closer than 10 m. For safety reasons, trenches should not be more than 4 feet (1.2 m) deep. If trenches must exceed this depth, the SWCA team will follow Office of Safety and Health Administration regulations by stepping back one side of the trench, excavating access and egress side trenches every 20 m along the trench, and/or shoring the trench with hydraulic safety equipment.

Once the trench is excavated, both walls will be faced, using trowels and shovels to remove gouges and smeared soils and observe the deposits in profile. Features exposed in a trench will be documented by profiling, describing, and photographing them. Feature locations and profiles will be tied into the site Cartesian grid and elevation datum. Unproductive trenches will be refilled as soon as possible for logistical and safety reasons.

Once the site stratigraphy (if any) has been defined through the vertical exposures in trenches, horizontal mechanical stripping can be done with far greater sensitivity to pit feature–use surface relationships. Where post-abandonment deposits are present over and within prehistoric features, a special 4-foot-wide bucket can be used to strip away sediments. The wide bucket allows the sediments to be removed in consecutive, overlapping cuts only a few centimeters thick, leaving a smooth exposure that allows the monitoring archaeologist to examine the deposits and identify any cultural features not exposed by trenching. For example, palisades are much more likely to be identified in horizontal exposures than in the few initial trenches.

Excavation of Architectural Features

Excavation of architectural features will focus on recovering (1) detailed architectural information, including structural details, construction techniques, and remodeling events, (2) stratigraphic data that relate to abandonment and post-abandonment processes (including any evidence of reoccupation), and (3) associated artifacts and samples, including datable materials such as tree-ring, radiocarbon, and archaeomagnetic samples. Of the various architectural remains exposed during the project, SWCA expects PI pit structures to be the richest source of behavioral information, as habitation activities were intensive in these structures, and preservation will be better than in surface rooms or on extramural surfaces. All pit structures in the project area will be at least sampled to recover basic architectural, stratigraphic, and artifact data. A sample of structures will be more fully excavated because of their importance as sources of data

relevant to Problem Domain III of the prehistoric research design. Exposed pit structures that show evidence of burning will be investigated further to facilitate the recovery of preserved (carbonized) tree-ring samples.

Initially, a backhoe trench will be excavated into the fill of each pit structure or suspected pit structure to just above the floor, allowing a quick and efficient exposure of the pit dimensions, the fill sequence, remodeling events, and the feature's potential to yield tree-ring samples for dendrochronological analysis. Once the floor is exposed either mechanically or by hand in the trench, a detailed profile of the fill will be drawn, exposed floor features such as hearths will be sampled, and a control unit will be hand excavated off the trench to retrieve artifact samples from exposed strata. This strategy will permit a large number of pit structures to be sampled quickly and intensively for data relevant to the research design and allow highly informed selection of pit structures for further excavation. Pit structures selected for further excavation will be excavated mechanically to 10 cm above the feature floor (or roof remains if present), and then by hand to retrieve tree-ring samples if appropriate wood is present and any floor-associated artifacts. Floor fill deposits will be screened through 1/4-inch wire mesh (unless fill deposits indicate finer screening would be beneficial and productive). All artifacts in contact with a floor surface will be point located, individually collected, and drawn on the final structure map. Any floor features present will be mapped and sampled. At least one half of each structure selected for further excavation will be excavated in this way.

Surface rooms in the project area tend to be truly superficial and thus poorly preserved (Fuller 1988b). However, some surface rooms excavated during other projects have had intact clay floors. The excavation of surface rooms will have two objectives: (1) defining the horizontal extent and nature of surface architecture and (2) exposing intact surfaces from which to recover artifacts and micro-artifact and floor samples. These data will help determine the sizes and functions of surface rooms associated with each household unit. Any associated artifacts or clay samples recovered will be fully analyzed. Any stratigraphy or subfeatures that are encountered will be treated in the same way as pit structure contexts.

Electronic forms will be completed, summarizing the excavation of each room, documenting the various levels of excavation, and detailing the architectural and depositional characteristics of each feature. Plan view drawings will be produced for all structures, showing at a minimum the walls of the room, the lines used to define the room quarters or halves, the location of all floor samples, artifacts, and subfeatures, the location of disturbances and intact plastered areas or other notable floor characteristics, and the location and orientation of profile lines. Each feature will also be digitally photographed from more than one angle and during various stages of the excavation. All digital forms and graphical representations will be linked to the project GIS database.

Excavation of Extramural Areas and Other Features

The sampling strategy for extramural features such as middens, plazas or ramadas, palisades/stockades, and non-architectural pit features will vary considerably depending on the nature of the data they can yield with respect to the research design.

Middens provide a wealth of data on subsistence, artifacts, discard behavior, site structure, site chronology, and site use-life. One of the challenges of midden excavation is knowing when a sample is representative. To generate a sample that is statistically representative of prehistoric household middens, randomly placed excavation units will be excavated in each midden. As it is the sample size and the unbiased collection of those samples that matters, not sample proportion, the extent to which middens are sampled will depend on the artifact sample sizes that they yield. If one excavation unit does not yield sufficient numbers of artifacts to address research concerns, additional randomly placed units will be excavated. This sampling procedure ensures not only that the range of variability within a midden is characterized, but also that the sample is statistically random so that the data can be used in accumulations studies, which can provide information on the site's occupation duration (Varien and Potter 1997). If a midden feature is small and does not yield large numbers of artifacts, the entire feature may be excavated.

Excavation of midden areas will be completed by randomly establishing excavation units within the midden

boundaries. The most common unit sizes will be 1 × 1 m. Excavation of the units will proceed in either 10-cm or 20-cm arbitrary levels, unless strata can be identified. Midden fill will be sifted through 1/4- or 1/8-inch screens. If strata are identified, a stratigraphic profile will be drawn and digitally photographed.

Many PI household units have evidence of ramadas or activity areas between the surface rooms and the pit structure. Hand units may be excavated in this area of a sample of unit pueblos to expose features such as post holes and pits and to recover artifacts and samples from the identified activity areas.

If more formal plaza areas are identified, a more flexible approach is required, adapting the sampling effort to the specifics of the occupation and post-abandonment formation processes associated with the plaza. The primary goals of excavations in formal plaza areas will be to identify the actual plaza surface or surfaces (if preserved) and to expose associated features and in situ artifacts. If a plaza is surrounded by room block architecture, fallen stone will often have preserved portions of the edges of the surface. Hand-excavation units may thus be excavated along the edges of these features, as well as toward the center.

Stockades/palisades may exist around some sites in the project area. Hand and mechanical stripping will be employed around each habitation to expose evidence of enclosing architecture. Any post holes thus exposed will be fully documented and investigated for the possible collection of tree-ring samples.

Excavation of Inhumations

In archaeology, it is sometimes necessary to expose the remains of deceased human beings. Excavation, analysis, and reporting of human remains will always be conducted in a respectful and professional manner, and will be performed only by experienced personnel. The remains will not be publicly displayed and will be treated with reverence, respect, and care by all employees at all times. Human remains will not be left exposed overnight or over a weekend. Any burial that is encountered late in the day or late in the work week will not be further exposed; instead, the remains will be covered with culturally sterile earth, the refilled burial will be topped with plastic to protect it from rain, and the burial will be camouflaged until it can be fully excavated in one day. These efforts will help disguise the feature if unauthorized persons visit a site while the crew is absent.

Once the upper extent of a burial pit is identified, the pit will be excavated in natural or arbitrary levels. Burial pit fill is often simply a single mixed deposit of construction fill and/or midden deposits that was placed over the individual after the burial, and in such cases the backfill material can be excavated as a single stratum and level. Fill from a burial pit will be screened through 1/4-inch wire mesh until the remains are encountered, at which point all remaining fill (including sediments around and under the remains) will be screened with 1/8-inch wire mesh.

If multiple inhumations are found within a single burial pit, each individual will be given a separate feature number, so that the number of individuals in the mortuary population is adequately represented. In such cases, the bulk of the burial pit fill will be related to the most recent interment in the pit. For multiple individuals, the fill excavated from the area immediately around each individual will be assigned to the feature number for that individual burial.

If vessels are found as funerary offerings, their contents will be removed only in the laboratory, unless preservation factors dictate otherwise. Appropriate samples may be collected from various proveniences within a burial, as dictated by the nature of the individual feature (or as stipulated by the plan of work, agency regulations, or the project Memorandum of Agreement). Pollen samples may be recovered from the cranial, abdominal, and pelvic regions, and from around or within associated funerary items. Forms detailing the characteristics of the burial and the osteological attributes of the individual will be completed for each burial, and plan-view and cross-section drawings will be generated.

All human remains will be carefully wrapped and packaged in the field for maximum protection and transported to the project laboratory as soon as possible to prevent breakage and deterioration. Human remains will not be wrapped with aluminum foil or in cotton batting. Paper products such as bags, newspapers, and paper towels or tissue are generally acceptable. All remains will be securely placed in boxes during transportation and storage. Within the boxes, cotton batting may be used to pad remains that are in paper containers. Processing and analysis will be implemented as soon as possible upon the arrival of the remains at the laboratory. Neither human remains nor associated funerary items from the ALP project will leave the State of Colorado at any time.

Archaeobotanical and Dating Sample Collection

The recovery of archaeobotanical and dating samples is integral to all three problem domains in the research design. The more common types of samples collected during excavations and the methods to be used for each are briefly described here.

Botanical

Specific strategies for the collection of botanical samples, both microbotanical (pollen, phytolith, and starch) and macrobotanical (macrofloral and flotation), will be fine-tuned in consultation with the Archaeobotanical Director before the start of fieldwork. Additional refinements are likely as the initial results trickle in.

Flotation and pollen samples will always be collected in tandem, to provide complementary data on each sampled context. At least one set of samples will be collected and analyzed from each major feature and deposit. Special emphasis will be placed on collecting samples from contexts such as structure floors, features that exhibit rapid fill sequences, and the interiors of vessels. When selecting the samples for actual analysis, factors to be considered include type of context, integrity of the deposits that were sampled, and uniqueness or redundancy of the sample.

Sampling of structures is a special concern. At a minimum, for every pit or surface room, one set of samples will be recovered from the floor exposed in the control unit. If sealed contexts (e.g., beneath floor artifacts) or other optimum sampling locations are not identified, composite samples will be collected from three to six points across the sampled area. In addition, the fill of pit structures and floor features will be sampled.

Flotation samples will be collected to recover macrobotanical remains of economic plant species, such as corn cobs or kernels, beans, squash seeds or rind fragments, and wild plant seeds, berries, and other fragments. Ideally, flotation samples from features and subfeatures will consist of at least 2 liters of sediment recovered from a single, unmixed, undisturbed context. When the fill from a sampled feature is less than 2 liters, a pollen sample will be collected first. The remaining fill will be collected as a flotation sample, and the approximate volume of the sample will be indicated on the sample forms. Flotation samples will be placed in clean doubled paper bags to prevent mold and mildew during storage.

Contexts that have burned and that reflect the function of the feature are the best areas for recovery of flotation samples. Unburned botanical remains do not preserve well in open-air sites, and unburned materials in a flotation sample are generally considered to be intrusive and are not studied.

If significant deposits of macrobotanical materials are encountered, they will be separated from regular flotation samples. Items such as burned matting, textiles, wooden artifacts, and stored economic materials such as corn will be carefully packaged and submitted to the laboratory as botanical samples. Radiocarbon samples may also be retained from these materials. If macrobotanical remains are present even after botanical and radiocarbon samples have been recovered, the remainder may be submitted as an additional flotation sample.

Pollen samples will consist of at least 4–6 tablespoons of sediment from a given provenience. Each sediment sample will be collected from a freshly exposed soil surface and immediately placed in a self-sealing plastic bag. Pollen samples will be collected from the bottommost fill of all thermal features, such as hearths, fire pits, ash pits, and roasting pits. Slab-lined pits and granary pedestals will also be rigorously sampled.

Pollen samples recovered from sealed contexts on floors, such as beneath metates or smashed vessels, securely reflect the pollen on the floor when that floor was in use. Such samples, as well as pollen washes of in situ ground stone items, will be collected in addition to the composite floor samples. Pollen washes are often recovered from manos; these artifacts will be sealed as soon as possible, and the surface that was in contact with the floor will be marked in some manner. Wrapping a pollen-wash artifact in a foil pouch and marking the upper and lower faces of the tool with masking tape on the foil is an adequate means of preservation. Pollen samples from metates can consist of sediment samples from the fill adjacent to the grinding surface.

Where phytolith analysis is indicated, the phytoliths are recovered from the sediments collected as pollen samples. This analysis is similar in some respects to pollen identification but examines tiny silica-based plant structures that can be used to identify species. Field personnel do not have to be concerned with these samples, except to be sure to recover enough material (4–6 tablespoons) to permit both pollen and phytolith analysis.

Radiocarbon

Conventional radiocarbon samples will always be collected when sufficient amounts of charcoal are present. Annual plant remains such as corn cobs or kernels, juniper berries, and piñon cones or nuts, as well as artifacts such as matting or textiles made from annual materials, provide the best samples for conventional radiocarbon dating. Annual materials most likely will represent a specific year, or a narrow range of years, during the occupation of a structure, whereas wood charcoal can derive from wood that had been dead many decades before it was collected for use.

Conventional radiocarbon samples will not be touched with bare hands and will be packaged in aluminum foil for storage before analysis. The sample records will detail the context and probable origin of the charcoal.

Where large pieces or amounts of charcoal are not recovered, AMS dating of small bits of charcoal is the best alternative. A single small cob fragment (or other identifiable fragment of an annual species) can suffice. In addition, project ethnobotanists can be alerted to save out identifiable maize or other fragments from a flotation sample for submission for AMS dating.

When all else fails, it is possible to conduct AMS dating on the charcoal dust from culturally stained soil (Phillips and Polk 2001).

In a context where a radiocarbon date is desirable but where direct sampling is not possible and flotation-derived samples are unlikely (the soil is stained, but individual bits of charred material are not evident), the field crew can collect the necessary sample by filling a one-gallon ziplock bag with the stained soil. This bulk sample is then submitted to the radiocarbon laboratory for extraction and dating of the charcoal dust.

Dendrochronology

The SWCA team expects to collect numerous tree-ring samples, given the abundance of structural features in the project area and the local use of datable species for structural wood. Juniper is occasionally datable, piñon pine is better, and ponderosa pine and other tall conifers are best. If the outer portion of a beam or post fragment is preserved and has some 50 or more rings, at least one sample will be collected from that beam or post; the ideal will be to recover a complete cross section. Tree-ring samples will be wrapped in cotton string, then aluminum foil, and placed in clean, dry paper bags. The old practice of soaking the post in a solution of paraffin and gasoline poses serious health and safety concerns, is rarely used today, and will not be used during the ALP project.

Archaeomagnetic

Archaeomagnetic analysis has become a primary dating method and is applied whenever such samples can be collected. Most archaeomagnetic samples derive from hearths, but burned clay-plastered floors, walls, and storage features can be sampled as well. Under certain conditions, water-laid clay lenses in canals and reservoirs can also be dated in this way. For habitation features, archaeomagnetic dates from hearths usually reflect the terminal use of a feature, which, combined with dates on construction materials, indicates the use-life of the habitation. For all these reasons, archaeomagnetic sampling will be a component of the chronometric studies for the ALP project.

Admittedly, the dating curve for the Southwest is highly convoluted, and samples can yield multiple dates. In such cases, though, other dating methods can be used to rule out alternative dates, and the remaining acceptable date can be combined with the other chronological information to refine the dating of a feature. Another limitation of archaeomagnetic dating is the lack of an interpretive curve for much of the human occupation of the region that includes Ridges Basin. However, the ALP project is in a position to help extend the curve, if we can obtain Archaic or BMII archaeomagnetic samples in conjunction with radiocarbon or tree-ring samples.

SAMPLING DESIGN

The sampling design is intended to facilitate the retrieval of data relevant to the questions posed in the ALP research design. Given the real-world constraints of time and budgets, it is not possible to completely excavate every site in the project area. However, it is possible to develop strategies that allow the recovery of large amounts of important archaeological data within the designated project parameters. The reality is that extensive archaeology will be conducted as part of this project, and it is essential to develop a strategy for allocating effort and resources that will maximize the amount of data pertinent to addressing the research design.

Within the sample universe of sites eligible for the NRHP in the project area (ca. 100) and that will be impacted by either reservoir filling or construction is a range of prehistoric site-types that includes Pueblo habitation sites, small structural sites, and artifact scatters. All protohistoric and historic sites will be investigated as outlined in their respective research designs. The following sampling strategy for each prehistoric site type describes both how sites will be selected for excavation and, once they are selected, how they will be excavated.

Pueblo Habitation Sites

All PI habitation sites will be selected for at least sample excavation. Since the crux of the prehistoric research design related to the Puebloan period depends on establishing momentary population estimates for the project area, the primary information needed from these sites will be the number of pit houses present on a site and their dates and duration of occupation. To obtain these data, Phase I data recovery on these sites will consist of (1) excavating a backhoe trench and a hand-excavated control unit to the floor in every suspected pit structure,

(2) sample-excavating all middens to obtain representative household artifact assemblages, and (3) excavating a hand unit in suspected room block architecture.

This strategy will provide data from every habitation site on:

- the number of pit houses or pit structures on a site;

- the post-abandonment profile of each pit structure;

- artifacts and samples in the post-abandonment fill of pit structures;

- some architectural information on structure dimensions and wall and floor construction;

- chronological information, including ^{14}C samples from post-abandonment fill and potentially from hearths as well, tree-ring samples, ceramic assemblages, and archaeomagnetic samples;

- remodeling events in the form of multiple floors, if present;

- household activities, chronology, economy, subsistence, and occupation duration from midden deposits; and

- the potential for any given feature to provide additional information relevant to the research design.

It is important to stress that data obtained during Phase I investigations will be the most important information for addressing the research design questions.

Phase II data recovery will be conducted on a sample of habitation sites and will consist primarily of more extensive excavation, such as exposing the floors of pit structures or excavating extramural areas or surface architectural features more extensively. The selection of these sites will relate to their capacity to provide data crucial to addressing the research design, including information on architectural variation, activity variation within and among structures, household abandonment and occupation duration (e.g., evidence of remodeling), settlement structure, and chronology. Many of these factors will depend on the preservation of structures, the complexity of the site structure, and whether there are burned structures on a site, which increases the chance of recovering dendrochronological samples.

The primary advantage of this two-phased strategy is that economic, abandonment, and chronological data will be recovered from every habitation structure in the project area, supplemented with architectural and morphological data from a selected sample of sites. This strategy of trenching every pit structure to obtain baseline data from as many habitation structures as possible was successfully employed at Grass Mesa Village as part of the Dolores Archaeology Program and more recently by Crow Canyon Archaeology Center at the Shields Site (M. Varien, personal communication 2002).

Small Structural Sites

These sites are less numerous than habitation sites in the project area, and sample excavations will be conducted at all of them. The primary information required from these sites is chronological data and the range of associated activities. Data on architectural variation will be a secondary goal. To achieve these objectives, collecting artifacts and, secondarily, architectural data, will guide sampling procedures.

Artifact Scatters

Artifact scatters in the project area are highly diverse and include possible Archaic and BMII habitations and limited-activity sites dating to all time periods. A strategy that ensures a representative sample of each type of artifact scatter will be important. Site selection will be based on the information potential of the site, the likely date of the site, and previous work at the site. Sites to be included in the sample are (1) those that appear to contain numerous artifacts and possibly multiple activity or temporal loci, (2) those that may date to the Archaic or BMII period, and/or (3) those where little or no previous work has been conducted. Sites that will likely be excluded from the sample are PI limited-activity sites that have been previously collected.

Sampling within artifact scatters will follow a stratified random strategy. Areas of artifact concentration will be randomly sampled, both on the surface with collection units and subsurface with hand units, until sufficient artifact numbers are obtained to characterize the sampling strata with statistical confidence. Subsurface features that are encountered will be mapped and may be excavated and sampled for datable and botanical materials. Subsurface testing of these sites using a backhoe stripping bucket will then be conducted, and additional features will be mapped and possibly excavated/sampled.

As indicated in the research design, a sample of nonceramic artifact scatters will be subjected to magnetometer or soil resistivity studies so that potential subsurface features and their associated surfaces may be located and hand excavated. CASA used this technique in 1986 to locate subsurface features on artifact scatters and found that is was fairly effective at identifying anomalies that may be features. Selection of sites for this analysis will depend on surface artifact types and densities and the geomorphology of particular sites and will be done in coordination with both the magnetometer/resistivity specialist and the project geomorphologist.

ARCHAEOLOGICAL FIELD LABORATORY

For the ALP project, SWCA will establish a complete laboratory facility in Durango with sufficient space for locked, temperature-controlled temporary storage of materials. As required by the contract, the proposed location of this facility will be submitted for advance approval.

The laboratory will house initial artifact processing (e.g., washing and drying of artifacts, flotation, sorting of artifacts, and initial preparation for curation) as well as more intensive analyses (such as faunal analysis). All processing and curation preparation will be done in accordance with Anasazi Heritage Center standards. Data from all levels of analysis and recording, from collection proveniences to specialized analyses, will be entered directly into a project database. SWCA will maintain or hire a local, full-time specialist staff to conduct analyses as the materials come out of processing. As part of its local hiring, SWCA plans to employ members of the Colorado Ute Tribes in the laboratory and provide them with on-the-job training. Danielle Desruisseaux will direct the laboratory, and all analyses will be conducted under the direction of the Project Director.

All analytical protocols will be interlinked using the project provenience system, so that all analyses of particular contexts can be compiled to address research topics involving those contexts. Both laboratory processing and analytical procedures will be explicitly coordinated through the project Quality Control Plan, with appropriately detailed laboratory and analytical manuals for constant reference by technicians and analysts. In addition, training programs for laboratory and analytical personnel will be developed, including specific plans for monitoring and maintaining analytical consistency throughout the multi-year project. Any analytical changes necessary during the course of the project will be structured to ensure continued comparability of data. Data files will be carefully checked and maintained, and adequately protected with separately stored backup files.

COMPUTER DATABASE

Over the past decade, SWCA has successfully built and maintained computer databases for multiple excavation projects, and we have an experienced Information Technology and GIS staff to assist in their design and operation. For the ALP project, SWCA will use Microsoft Access to build a comprehensive database that will track proveniences, artifact inventories and analyses, photographs, graphics and maps, and field data. This relational database will be tied to a GIS product (detailed in the Analysis section of this document) that is provenience-based. Archaeological excavation data are well suited for this approach, as the data are both spatially and hierarchically organized.

Field excavations will be divided into provenience designations (PDs) based on the size and shape of the excavation unit. Each artifact class collected from each PD will be given a unique bag number, which will be entered directly into the project database. Laboratory personnel will then be able to track each bag from the field into the laboratory, then to analysis, and finally to curation by use of the bag number. Analysts will be able to tie these bags to their proveniences and associated assemblages through the PD. This system will facilitate ease of tracking as well as ease of artifact analysis and interpretation.

REFERENCES CITED

Adams, Karen R.

1978   A New Method for Quantitatively Evaluating Wild Plant Resources in the Rio Puerco Valley of New Mexico. Paper presented at the 43rd Annual Meeting of the Society for American Archaeology, Tucson.

1993   Carbonized Plant Remains. In *The Duckfoot Site, Vol. I, Descriptive Archaeology*, edited by Ricky R. Lightfoot and Mary C. Etzkorn, pp. 195–220. Crow Canyon Archaeological Center Occasional Papers No. 3. Cortez.

2001   Looking Back Through Time, Southwestern U.S.: Archaeobotany at the New Millennium. In *Ethnobiology at the Millennium, Past Promise and Future Prospects*, edited by Richard I. Ford, pp. 49–99. Anthropological Paper No. 91. Museum of Anthropology, University of Michigan, Ann Arbor.

Adams, Karen R., and Robert E. Gasser

1980   Plant Microfossils from Archaeological Sites: Research Considerations and Sampling Techniques and Approaches. *The Kiva* 45:293–300.

Adler, Michael A.

1989   Ritual Facilities and Social Integration in Non-ranked Societies. In *The Architecture of Social Integration in Prehistoric Pueblos*, edited by William Lipe and Michelle Hegmon, pp. 35–52. Occasional Paper No. 1. Crow Canyon Archaeological Center, Cortez.

1990   *Communities of Soils and Stone: An Archaeological Investigation of Population Aggregation among the Mesa Verde Region Anasazi, A.D. 900–1300*. Ph.D. dissertation, University of Michigan, Ann Arbor.

1994   Population Aggregation and the Anasazi Social Landscape: A View from the Four Corners. In *The Ancient Southwestern Community: Models and Methods for the Study of Prehistoric Social Organization*, edited by Wirt Wills and Robert Leonard, pp. 85–101. University of New Mexico Press, Albuquerque.

Adler, Michael A., and Mark D. Varien

1994   The Changing Face of Community in the Mesa Verde Region A.D. 1000–1300. In *Proceedings of the Anasazi Symposium 1991*, compiled by Jack Smith and Ann Hutchinson, pp. 83–97. Mesa Verde National Park, Mesa Verde.

Adler, Michael A., and Richard Wilshusen

1990   Large-scale Integrative Facilities in Tribal Societies: Cross-cultural and Southwestern Examples. *World Archaeology* 22:133–145.

Ahlstrom, Richard V.

1985   *The Interpretation of Archaeological Tree-Ring Dates*. Ph.D. dissertation, University of Arizona, Tucson.

Allison, James R.

1995   *Early Puebloan Ceramics*. Animas–La Plata Archaeological Project Research Paper No. 3. Northern Arizona University, Flagstaff.

2000   *Craft Specialization and Exchange in Small-Scale Societies: A Virgin Anasazi Case Study*. Ph.D. dissertation, Department of Anthropology, Arizona State University, Tempe.

Baker, Steven G.

1983a   Current Research, Northern Plains and Mountain States. *SHA Newsletter* 16(4):36–38. Society for Historical Archaeology, Glassboro, New Jersey.

1983b   Historical Archaeology in the Ridgeway Reservoir, Ouray County, Colorado: An Overview of Resources, Contribution Potentials and Current Program Status. In *Forgotten Places and Things: Archaeological Perspectives on American History*, compiled and edited by Albert E. Ward, pp. 75–83. Contributions to Anthropological Studies No. 3. Center for Anthropological Studies, Albuquerque.

1983c   The Railroad and the American Victorian Cultural Horizon: An Archaeological Perspective from Colorado. In *Forgotten Places and Things: Archaeological Perspectives on American History*, compiled and edited by Albert E. Ward, pp.

239–249. Contributions to Anthropological Studies No. 3. Center for Anthropological Studies, Albuquerque.

1986   Current Research, Northern Plains and Mountain States. *Society for Historical Archaeology Newsletter* 19(1):37.

1988   Current Research, Northern Plains and Mountain States. *Society for Historical Archaeology Newsletter* 21(3):36–37.

1990   Current Research, Northern Plains and Mountain States. *Society for Historical Archaeology Newsletter* 23(2):40–41.

1996   Current Research, Northern Plains and Mountain States. *Society for Historical Archaeology Newsletter* 29(4):21–22.

Ballagh, Jean H., and John D. Goodman II
1999   Historic Period Demography. In *The Carlota Copper Mine Archaeological Project, Volume 6: Summary and Synthesis*, by Douglas R. Mitchell, John D. Goodman II, Jean H. Ballagh, and Chris T. Wenker, pp. 7-1 to 7-21. (Draft Final Report) SWCA Archaeological Report No. 97-191. Flagstaff.

Bassett, Everett
1994   "We Took Care of Each Other Like Families Were Meant To": Gender, Social Organization, and Wage Labor among the Apache at Roosevelt. In *Those of Little Note: Gender, Race, and Class in Historical Archaeology*, edited by Elizabeth M. Scott, pp. 55–79. University of Arizona Press, Tucson.

Baugh, Timothy G.
1989   Historical Literature Search, Porter Mines, La Plata County, Colorado. In *Ridges Basin Reservoir Geologic Design Data Report G-500, Volume 2, Appendices 2, 3, and 4*. USDI Bureau of Reclamation, Durango Projects Office, Durango.

Baxter, Michael
1994   *Exploratory Multivariate Analysis in Archaeology*. Edinburgh University Press, Edinburgh.

Bennett, Connie, and John Weymouth
1986   Final Report of Magnetic Survey of Ridges Basin Archaeological Sites in the Animas–La Plata Project, Colorado. In *The Cultural Resources of Ridges Basin and Upper Wildcat Canyon*, edited by Joseph C. Winter, John A. Ware, and Philip J. Arnold III, pp. 365–530. Office of Contract Archeology, University of New Mexico, Albuquerque.

Billman, Brian R.
1997   *The Archaic Period Occupation of the Ute Mountain Ute Piedmont*. Publications in Archaeology No. 21. Soil Systems, Inc., Phoenix.

Binford, Lewis R.
1980   Willow Smoke and Dog's Tails: Hunter-Gatherer Settlement Systems and Site Formation. *American Antiquity* 45(1):4–20.

Blackaby, James R., and Patricia Greeno (editors)
1988   *The Revised Nomenclature for Museum Cataloging: A Revised and Expanded Version of Robert G. Chenhall's System for Classifying Man-Made Objects*. AASLH Press, Nashville.

Blinman, Eric
1986   Exchange and Interaction. In *Dolores Archaeological Program: Final Synthetic Report*, compiled by D. A. Breternitz, Christine K. Robinson, and G. Timothy Gross, pp. 53–101. USDI Bureau of Reclamation, Engineering and Research Center, Denver.

1988   *The Interpretation of Ceramic Variability: A Case Study from the Dolores Anasazi*. Ph.D. dissertation, Washington State University, Pullman.

1989   Potluck in the Protokiva: Ceramics and Ceremonialism in Pueblo I Villages. In *The Architecture of Social Integration in Prehistoric Pueblos*, edited by William Lipe and Michelle Hegmon, pp. 113–124. Occasional Paper No. 1. Crow Canyon Archaeological Center, Cortez.

Blinman, Eric, and C. Dean Wilson
1988   Overview of A.D. 600–800 Ceramic Production and Exchange in the Dolores Project Area. In

Dolores Archaeological Program, Supporting Studies: Additive and Reductive Technologies, compiled by Eric Blinman, Carl Phagan, and Richard Wilshusen, pp. 395–423. USDI Bureau of Reclamation, Engineering and Research Center, Denver.

Bohrer, Vorsila L., and Karen R. Adams
1977 Ethnobotanical Techniques and Approaches at Salmon Ruin, New Mexico. *Eastern New Mexico University Contributions in Anthropology* 8(1):1–215.

Bonan, Mark
1985 1965 Excavations: The Mike Bodo Project. In *Fort Lewis College Archaeological Investigations on Ridges Basin, Southwest Colorado, 1965-1982*, edited by Phil Duke, pp. 25–48. Occasional Papers of the Center for Southwest Studies No. 4. Fort Lewis College, Durango.

Breternitz, David A., Arthur H. Rohn, Jr., and Elizabeth A. Morris
1974 *Prehistoric Ceramics of the Mesa Verde Region.* Ceramic Series No. 5. Museum of Northern Arizona, Flagstaff.

Brew, John O.
1946 *Archaeology of Alkali Ridge, Southeastern Utah.* Papers of the Peabody Museum, Vol. 21. Harvard University, Cambridge.

Buckles, William G.
1986 *Old Dallas Historical Archaeological Program, Dallas Creek Project.* USDI Bureau of Reclamation, Upper Colorado Region, Salt Lake City.

Buckles, William G., and Nancy B. Buckles
1984 *Colorado Historical Archaeology Context.* Office of Archaeology and Historic Preservation, Colorado Historical Society, Denver.

Buikstra, Jane E., and Douglas H. Ubelaker (editors)
1994 *Standards for Data Collection from Human Skeletal Remains.* Arkansas Archaeological Survey Research Series No. 44. Fayetteville.

Carlson, Roy L.
1963 *Basket Maker III Sites near Durango, Colorado.* Studies in Anthropology No. 8. University of Colorado, Boulder.

Chenault, Mark
2002 The Micro-Archaeology of Hohokam Floors. In *Culture and Environment in the American Southwest: Essays in Honor of Robert C. Euler*, edited by David A. Phillips, Jr., and John A. Ware, pp. 89–112. SWCA Anthropological Research Paper No. 8, Phoenix.

Chenault, Mark L., and Thomas N. Motsinger
2000 Colonization, Warfare, and Regional Competition: Recent Research into the Basketmaker III Period in the Mesa Verde Region. In *Foundations of Anasazi Culture: The Basketmaker-Pueblo Transition*, edited by Paul F. Reed, pp. 45–65. University of Utah Press, Salt Lake City.

Chenhall, Robert G.
1978 *Nomenclature for Museum Cataloging: A System for Classifying Man-Made Objects.* American Association for State and Local History, Nashville.

Church, Minette
2000 Permeable Ethnic Boundaries on the Southern Colorado "Frontier." Paper presented at the 65th Annual Meeting of the Society for American Archaeology, Philadelphia.

Dean, Jeffrey
1975 *Tree-ring Dates from Colorado W – Durango Area.* Laboratory of Tree-ring Research, University of Arizona, Tucson.

Dishman, Linda
1982 Ranching and Farming in the Lower Dolores River Valley. In *The River of Sorrows: The History of the Lower Dolores River Valley*, edited by Gregory D. Kendrick, pp. 23–41. USDI National Park Service, Rocky Mountain Regional Office, Denver.

Duke, Philip G.
1985 *Fort Lewis College Archaeological Investigations in Ridges Basin, Southwest Colorado:*

1965–1982. Occasional Paper of the Center for Southwest Studies No. 4. Fort Lewis College, Durango.

Duke, Philip, and Gary Matlock
1999   *Points, Pit houses, and Pioneers: Tracing Durango's Archaeological Past.* University Press of Colorado, Miwot.

Duran, Meliha S., and C. Timothy McKeown
1980   Historic Artifacts. In *Prehistory and History of the Ojo Amarillo: Archaeological Investigations of Block II, Navajo Indian Irrigation Project, San Juan County, New Mexico*, vol. 3, edited by David T. Kirkpatrick, pp. 102–1208. Report No. 276. Cultural Resources Management Division, Sociology and Anthropology Department, New Mexico State University, Las Cruces.

Duranceau, Deborah A.
1983   Oral History as a Tool of Historical Archaeology: Application on the Dolores Archaeological Project. In *Forgotten Places and Things: Archaeological Perspectives on American History*, compiled and edited by Albert E. Ward, pp. 27–31. Contributions to Anthropological Studies No. 3. Center for Anthropological Studies, Albuquerque.

Eddy, Frank W., Allen E. Kane, and Paul R. Nickens
1984   *Southwest Colorado Prehistoric Context: Archaeological Background and Research Directions.* Office of Archaeology and Historic Preservation, Colorado Historical Society, Denver.

Ezzo, Joseph A., and T. Douglas Price
2002   Migration, Regional Reorganization, and Spatial Group Composition at Grasshopper Pueblo, Arizona. *Journal of Archaeological Science* 29:499–520.

Fetterman, Jerry E., and Linda Honeycutt
1982   *Testing and Excavation Report, MAPCO's Rocky Mountain Liquid Hydrocarbons Pipeline, Southwest Colorado.* Woods Canyon Archaeological Consultants, Yellowjacket, Colorado.

2001   Synthesis. In *Data Recovery of Three Sites along El Paso Field Services' Trunk N Pipeline, San Juan County, New Mexico,* edited by Jerry Fetterman, Jannifer Gish, Linda Honeycutt, Lisa Huckell, Lori Reed, Marian Rohman, Deb Silverman, Paul Stirniman, and John Torres, pp. 8-1 to 8-21. Woods Canyon Archaeological Consultants Project No. 2001-10. Yellowjacket, Colorado.

Fuller, Steven L.
1988a   *Cultural Resources Inventories for the Animas–La Plata Project. The Wheeler and Koshak Borrow Sources.* Four Corners Archaeological Project Report No. 12. Complete Archaeological Service Associates, Cortez.

1988b   *Archaeological Investigations in the Bodo Canyon Area, La Plata County, Colorado.* UMTRA Archaeological Report No. 25. Complete Archaeological Service Associates, Cortez.

1989   *Research Design and Data Recovery Plan for the Animas–La Plata Project.* Four Corners Archaeological Project Report No. 15. Complete Archaeological Service Associates, Cortez.

Gerhold, Maureen
1982   Eastern Capital and Frontier Initiative: The History of the Montezuma Valley Irrigation System. In *The River of Sorrows: The History of the Lower Dolores River Valley*, edited by Gregory D. Kendrick, pp. 43–56. USDI National Park Service, Rocky Mountain Regional Office, Denver.

Gilpin, Dennis
1987   The NP-1 Historic Component: An 1890-to-1915 Farm and Ranch on the North Ponil, Colfax County, New Mexico. Ms. on file, Philmont Museum, Philmont Scout Ranch, Cimarron, New Mexico.

1993   Historical Archaeology on the Navajo Indian Irrigation Project. *DÁÁ'ÁK'EH NITSAA: An Overview of the Cultural Resources of the Navajo Indian Irrigation Project,* by Lawrence E. Vogler, Kristin Langenfeld, and Dennis

Gilpin, pp. 191–281. Navajo Nation Papers in Anthropology No. 29. Navajo Nation Archaeology Department, Window Rock, Arizona.

Gilpin, Dennis, and C. Timothy McKeown
1983 Historic Sites Laboratory Methods. In *Human Adaptation and Cultural Change: The Archaeology of Block III, Navajo Indian Irrigation Project*, edited by Lawrence E. Vogler, pp. 1199–1218. Navajo Nation Papers in Anthropology No. 15, Vol. 3. Navajo Nation Cultural Resource Management Program, Window Rock, Arizona.

Gilpin, Dennis, Randal R. Fox, and John A. Ware
1999 *Archaeological Testing on Navajo Route 9652.* SWCA Cultural Resources Report No. 99–258. Flagstaff.

Gladwin, Harold S.
1957 *A History of the Ancient Southwest.* The Bond Wheelwright Co., Portland, Maine.

Gooding, John D.
1980 *The Durango South Project: Archaeological Salvage of Two Late Basketmaker III Sites in the Durango District.* Anthropological Papers of the University of Arizona No. 34. University of Arizona Press, Tucson.

Goodman, Alan H., R. Brooke Thomas, Alan C. Swedlund, and George J. Armelagos
1988 Biocultural Perspectives on Stress in Prehistoric, Historical, and Contemporary Population Research. *Yearbook of Physical Anthropology* 31:169–202.

Grayson, Donald K.
1984 *Quantitative Zooarchaeology.* Academic Press, New York.

Gregg, Susan A., and Francis E. Smiley (editors)
1995 *Studies in Ridges Basin Archaeology.* Animas-La Plata Archaeological Project Research Paper No. 4. Northern Arizona University, Flagstaff.

Gregg, Susan A., Francis E. Smiley, and Lisa Folb (editors)
1995 *Archaeological Sites and Surfaces.* Animas–La Plata Archaeological Project Research Paper No. 1. Northern Arizona University, Flagstaff.

Hill, David
1988 Characterization of Ute Occupations and Ceramics from Southwestern Colorado. In *Archaeology of the Eastern Ute: A Symposium,* edited by P.R. Nickens, pp. 62-78. Occasional Papers No. 1. Colorado Council of Professional Archaeologists, Denver.

History Committee of the Fort Lewis Mesa Reunion
1994 *Pioneers of Southwest La Plata County, Colorado.* Family History Publishers, Salt Lake City.

Hogan, Patrick
1985 Foragers to Farmers: The Adoption of Agriculture in Northwestern New Mexico. Paper presented at the 50th Annual Meeting of the Society for American Archaeology, Denver.

1986 Overview, Research Design, and Data Recovery Program for Cultural Resources within *the Bolack Exchange Lands.* Office of Contract Archeology, University of New Mexico, Albuquerque.

Hogan, Patrick, Janette M. Elyea, and Peter N. Eschman
1991 *Overview and Research Design for the Fruitlands Coal and Gas Development Area.* Office of Contract Archeology, University of New Mexico, Albuquerque.

Horn, Jonathon C.
1986 *Archaeological Testing at Historic Site 5LP357, La Plata County, Colorado.* Nickens and Associates, Montrose.

1994 *Analysis of Artifacts from Sites 5MT10969 and 5MV3966, Montezuma County and Mesa Verde National Park, Colorado.* On file, Mesa Verde National Park, Research and Cultural Resources Management. Alpine Archaeological Consultants, Inc., Montrose.

1999   *Structural Stabilization at Animas Forks (5SA153), San Juan County, Colorado, 1997 and 1998 Field Seasons*. On file, Colorado Historical Society, Denver. Alpine Archaeological Consultants, Inc., Montrose.

Horn, Jonathan C., Jerry Fetterman, and Linda Honeycutt
2003   *The Mid-America Pipeline Company/Williams Rocky Mountain Expansion Loop Pipeline Data Recovery Project, Northwestern New Mexico, Western Colorado, and Eastern Utah. Volume 3: Colorado Technical Site Reports*. Alpine Archaeological Consultants, Inc., Montrose, Colorado, and Woods Canyon Archaeological Consultants, Yellowjacket, Colorado. Prepared for Williams, Tulsa.

Horn, Jonathon C., Gary Matlock, and Duane Smith
1984   *An Archaeological and Historical Investigation of an Historic Cabin at Site 5LP1252*. Nickens and Associates, Montrose.

1986   Archaeological Investigations of an Historic Cabin near Durango, Colorado. *Southwestern Lore* 52(3):1–33.

Huckell, Bruce B.
1995   *Of Marshes and Maize: Preceramic Agricultural Settlements in the Cienega Valley, Southeastern Arizona*. Anthropological Papers of the University of Arizona No. 59. Tucson.

Irwin-Williams, Cynthia
1973   *The Oshara Tradition: Origins of the Anasazi Culture*. Contributions in Anthropology Vol. 1, No. 2. Eastern New Mexico University, Portales.

1979   Post-Pliestocene Archaeology, 7000–2000 B.C. In *Southwest*, edited by Alfonso Ortiz, pp. 31–42. Handbook of North American Indians, Vol. 9, W. C. Sturtevant, general editor. Smithsonian Institution, Washington, D.C.

Jones, Volney H., and Robert L. Fonner
1954   Appendix C: Plant Materials from Sites in the Durango and La Plata Areas, Colorado. In *Basketmaker II Sites near Durango, Colorado*, by

Earl H. Morris and Robert F. Burgh, pp. 93–115. Publication No. 604. Carnegie Institute, Washington, D.C.

Kane, Alan E.
1986   Prehistory of the Dolores River Valley. In *Dolores Archaeological Program: Final Synthetic Report*, compiled by D. A. Breternitz, C. K. Robinson, and G. T. Gross, pp. 353–435. USDI Bureau of Reclamation, Engineering and Research Center, Denver.

Kendrick, Gregory D. (editor)
1982   *The River of Sorrows: The History of the Lower Dolores River Valley*. USDI National Park Service, Rocky Mountain Regional Office, Denver.

Kennedy, Kenneth A. R.
1983   Morphological Variations in Ulnar Supinator Crests and Fossae as Identifying Markers of Occupational Stress. *American Journal of Forensic Science* 28(4):871–876.

1989   Skeletal Markers of Occupational Stress. In *Reconstruction of Life from the Skeleton*, edited by M. Y. Iscan and K. A. R. Kennedy, pp. 12–160. Alan R. Liss, Inc., New York.

1998   Markers of Occupational Stress: Conspectus and Prognosis of Research. *International Journal of Osteoarchaeology* 8(5):305–311.

Klein, Richard, and Kathryn Cruz-Uribe
1984   *The Analysis of Animal Bones from Archaeological Sites*. University of Chicago Press, Chicago.

Leiby, Austin Nelson
1984   *Borderland Pathfinders: The 1765 Diaries of Juan María Antonio Rivera*. Ph.D. dissertation, Department of History, Northern Arizona University, Flagstaff.

Leidy, Kent
1976   *Archaeological Resources of the Animas–La Plata Project: Report of the 1975 Season*. Prepared for Interagency Archaeological Services, National Park Service. University of Colorado, Boulder.

Lekson, Steven H.
1991 Settlement Patterns and the Chaco Region. In *Chaco and Hohokam: Prehistoric Regional Systems in the American Southwest,* edited by Patricia L. Crown and W. James Judge, pp. 31–55. School of American Research Press, Santa Fe.

Lightfoot, Ricky R.
1994 *The Duckfoot Site, Vol. 2: Archaeology of the House and Household.* Occasional Paper No. 4. Crow Canyon Archaeological Center, Cortez.

Limerick, Patricia Nelson, Clyde A. Milner II, and Charles E. Rankin (editors)
1991 *Trails: Toward a New Western History.* University Press of Kansas, Lawrence.

Lipe, William D.
1994 Material Expression of Social Power in the Northern San Juan, A.D. 1150–1300. Paper presented at the Annual Meeting of the Society for American Archaeology, Anaheim.

1999 Basketmaker II (1000 B.C.–A.D. 500). In *Colorado Prehistory: A Context for the Southern Colorado River Basin,* edited by William D. Lipe, Mark D. Varien, and Richard H. Wilshusen, pp. 132–165. Colorado Council of Professional Archaeologists, Denver.

Lipe, William D., and Michelle Hegmon
1989 *The Architecture of Social Integration in Prehistoric Pueblos.* Occasional Paper No. 1. Crow Canyon Archaeological Center, Cortez.

Lipe, William D., and Bonnie L. Pitblado
1999 PaleoIndian and Archaic Periods. In *Colorado Prehistory: A Context for the Southern Colorado River Basin,* edited by William D. Lipe, Mark D. Varien, and Richard H. Wilshusen, pp. 95–131. Colorado Council of Professional Archaeologists, Denver.

Lipe, William D., Mark D. Varien, and Richard H. Wilshusen
1999 *Colorado Prehistory: A Context for the Southern Colorado River Basin.* Colorado Council of Professional Archaeologists, Denver.

Lyman, R. Lee
1994 *Vertebrate Taphonomy.* Cambridge University Press, Cambridge.

Mahoney, Nancy
1998 Beyond Bis Sa'ani: Rethinking the Scale and Organization of Great House Communities. Paper presented at the 63rd Annual Meeting of the Society for American Archaeology, Seattle.

Martin, Alexander C., and William D. Barkley
1961 *Seed Identification Manual.* University of California Press, Berkeley.

Martin, Debra L., and Alan H. Goodman
1995 Demography, Diet, and Disease in the Transitional Basketmaker III/Pueblo I Period. In *Studies in Ridges Basin Archaeology,* edited by Susan A. Gregg and Francis E. Smiley, pp. 1–44. Animas–La Plata Archaeological Project Research Paper No. 4. Northern Arizona University, Flagstaff.

Matson, R. G.
1991 *The Origins of Southwestern Agriculture.* University of Arizona Press, Tucson.

Matson, R. G., William D. Lipe, and William R. Haase
1988 Adaptational Continuities and Occupational Discontinuities: The Cedar Mesa Anasazi. *Journal of Field Archaeology* 15:245–264.

Mausolf, Lisa
1982 McPhee, Colorado: A 20th Century Lumber Company Town. In *The River of Sorrows: The History of the Lower Dolores River Valley,* edited by Gregory D. Kendrick, pp. 57–74. USDI National Park Service, Rocky Mountain Regional Office, Denver.

McKeown, C. Timothy
1983 Historic Artifacts: Materials and Manufacturing Technology. In *Human Adaptation and Cultural Change: The Archaeology of Block III, Navajo Indian Irrigation Project,* edited by Lawrence E. Vogler, pp. 1219–1368. Navajo Nation Papers in Anthropology No. 15, Vol. 3. Navajo Nation Cultural Resource Management Program, Window Rock, Arizona.

Merbs, Charles F.

1983 *Patterns of Activity-Induced Pathology in a Canadian Inuit Population.* National Museum of Man Mercury Series, Archaeological Survey of Canada Paper No. 119. Ottawa.

Miller, C. W.

1992 *Demographic Characteristics of the Population in the Mineral Industry of La Plata County, Colorado.* Copy on file, Durango Projects Office, Bureau of Reclamation, Durango.

Mills, Barbara J., Christine E. Goetze, and Maria Nieves Zedeño

1993 *Interpretation of Ceramic Artifacts.* Across the Colorado Plateau, Anthropological Studies for the Transwestern Pipeline, Vol. 16. Office of Contract Archeology, University of New Mexico, Albuquerque.

Minnis, Paul E.

1987 Identification of Wood from Archaeological Sites in the American Southwest, I: Keys for Gymnosperms. *Journal of Archaeological Science* 14:121–131.

Molleson, Theya

1994 The Eloquent Bones of Abu Hureya. *Scientific American* 31:70–75.

Morris, Earl H., and Robert F. Burgh

1954 Basketmaker II Sites near Durango, Colorado. Publication No. 604. Carnegie Institute, Washington, D.C.

Morris, James N.

1995 5LP-245: A Previously Excavated Early Puebloan Village. In *Archaeological Sites and Surfaces*, edited by Susan A. Gregg, Francis E. Smiley, and Lisa Folb, pp. 91–108. Animas–La Plata Archaeological Project Research Paper No. 1. Northern Arizona University, Flagstaff.

Murdock, G. P.

1949 *Social Structure.* Macmillan, New York.

Murray, Shawn S. and Karen R. Adams

2001 Identification Criteria Compendium. Contains descriptive materials and photos of all plant taxa and parts recovered from Crow Canyon Archaeological Sites. Ms. on file, Crow Canyon Archaeological Center, Cortez.

Nickens, Paul R.

1978 *Archaeological Resources on the La Plata River Drainage, Colorado and New Mexico: Cultural Resources Evaluation for the Animas La Plata Project.* Submitted to USDI Bureau of Reclamation, Upper Colorado Region, Salt Lake City. Centuries Research, Montrose.

Northern Arizona University and SWCA Environmental Consultants

1996 *Animas-La Plata Ethnographic Study.* Report submitted to the United States Department of Interior, Bureau of Reclamation, Upper Colorado Region.

Olin, Spencer C., Jr.

1986 Toward a Synthesis of the Political and Social History of the American West. *Pacific Historical Review* 55(4):599–611.

O'Rourke, Paul M.

1980 *Frontier in Transition: A History of Southwestern Colorado.* USDI Bureau of Land Management, Colorado State Office, Denver.

Perry, Elizabeth M.

2004 Archaeology of Labor and Gender in the Prehispanic American Southwest. Ph.D dissertation, University of Arizona, Tucson.

Phagan, Carl J., and G. Timothy Gross

1986 Reductive Technologies. In *Dolores Archaeological Program: Final Synthetic Report*, compiled by David Breternitz, Christine Robinson, and G. Timothy Gross, pp. 103–148. USDI Bureau of Reclamation, Engineering and Research Center, Denver.

Phagan, Carl J., and Richard Wilshusen

1988 Projectile Point Analysis, Part I: Production of Statistical Types and Subtypes. In *Dolores Archaeological Program: Supporting Studies: Additive and Reductive Technologies*, compiled by Eric Blinman, Carl Phagan, and Richard

Wilshusen, pp. 9–86. USDI Bureau of Reclamation, Engineering and Research Center, Denver.

Phillips, David A., Jr.
1996 *Cultural Resource Overview of Elephant Butte and Caballo Reservoirs, Sierra and Socorro Counties, New Mexico.* SWCA Archaeological Report No. 95-51. Albuquerque.

Phillips, David A., Jr., and Harding Polk II
2001 Dating the Undatable in Southeast New Mexico. Paper presented to the 2001 Jornada Mogollon Conference, Las Cruces.

Potter, James M.
1995 The Effects of Sedentism on the Processing of Hunted Carcasses in the American Southwest: A Comparison of Two Pueblo IV Sites in Central New Mexico. *Kiva* 60:411–428.

1997 Communal Ritual and Faunal Remains: An Example from the Dolores Anasazi. *Journal of Field Archaeology* 24:353–364.

2000 Pots, Parties, and Politics: Communal Feasting in the American Southwest. *American Antiquity* 65:471–492.

Prudden, T. Mitchell
1903 The Prehistoric Ruins in the San Juan Watershed in Utah, Arizona, Colorado, and New Mexico. *American Anthropologist* 5:224–288.

Reed, Alan D., and Jonathon C. Horn
1985 *Cultural Resource Monitoring of Construction of a Ski Lift Facility, Telluride, Colorado.* Nickens and Associates, Montrose.

Reher, Charles A. (editor)
1977 *Settlement and Subsistence along the Lower Chaco River: The CGP Survey.* University of New Mexico Press, Albuquerque.

Root, Homer
1967 Official Report of the Ridges Basin Project – Archaeological Field Work by Fort Lewis College. Homer Root Museum Objects Accession ledgers Volume 4. Durango CO: Collection M124, Robert Delaney Southwest Research

Library and Special Collections, Center for Southwest Studies, Fort Lewis College.

Rosillon, Mary P.
1984 *The Curecanti Archaeological Project: The Archeology of Marion, an Historic Railroad Camp in Curecanti National Recreation Area, Colorado.* Midwest Archeological Center Occasional Studies in Anthropology No. 9. Lincoln.

Schlanger, Sarah H., and Richard H. Wilshusen
1993 Local Abandonments and Regional Conditions in the North American Southwest. In *Abandonment of Settlements and Regions: Ethnoarchaeological and Archaeological Approaches*, edited by Cathy Cameron and Steve Tomka, pp. 85–98. Cambridge University Press, Cambridge.

Smiley, Francis E. (editor)
1995 *Lithic Assemblage Structure and Variation: Animas–La Plata Archaeological Project, 1992–1993 Investigations in Ridges Basin, Colorado.* Animas–La Plata Archaeological Project Research Paper No. 2. Northern Arizona University, Flagstaff.

Smiley, Francis E., and Lisa Folb (editors)
1997 *Animas La Plata Archaeological Project: A Research Summary and Assessment.* Animas–La Plata Archaeological Project Research Paper No. 6. Northern Arizona University, Flagstaff.

Smiley, Francis E., and Susan A Gregg (editors)
1995 *Cultural Dynamics and Transitions in the Northern Southwest: Animas–La Plata Archaeological Project, 1992 Research Design.* Animas–La Plata Archaeological Project Research Paper No. 5. Northern Arizona University, Flagstaff.

Smiley, Francis E., and Michael R. Robins
1997 *Early Farmers in the Northern Southwest: Papers on Chronometry, Social Dynamics, and Ecology.* Animas–La Plata Archaeological Project Research Paper No. 7. Northern Arizona University, Flagstaff.

Smith, Duane A.
1982 "Valley of the River of Sorrows": A Historical Overview of the Dolores River Valley. In *The*

River of Sorrows: The History of the Lower Dolores River Valley, edited by Gregory D. Kendrick, pp. 9–21. USDI National Park Service, Rocky Mountain Regional Office, Denver.

South, Stanley
1977   *Method and Theory in Historical Archaeology.* Academic Press, New York.

Sprague, Roderick
1981   A Functional Classification for Artifacts from 19th and 20th Century Historical Sites. *North American Archaeologist* 2(3):251–258.

Stein, Pat, and Jean Ballagh
1995   *A National Register Assessment of Historical Archaeological Resources for the Proposed Ridges Basin Reservoir, La Plata County, Colorado: The Animas La Plata Project.* SWCA Archaeological Report No. 95-10. Flagstaff.

Towner, Ronald H.
1997   *The Dendrochronology of the Navajo Pueblitos of the Dinétah.* Ph.D. dissertation, Department of Anthropology, University of Arizona, Tucson. University Microfilms, Ann Arbor.

Ubelaker, D. H.
1979   Skeletal Evidence for Kneeling in Prehistoric Ecuador. *American Journal of Physical Anthropology* 51:679–686.

Varien, Mark D.
1999   *Sedentism and Mobility in a Social Landscape: Mesa Verde and Beyond.* University of Arizona Press, Tucson.

Varien, Mark D., and Barbara J. Mills
1997   Accumulations Research: Problems and Prospects for Estimating Site Occupation Span. *Journal of Archaeological Method and Theory* 4:141–191.

Varien, Mark D., and James M. Potter
1997   Unpacking the Discard Equation: Simulating the Accumulation of Artifacts in the Archaeological Record. *American Antiquity* 62:194–213.

Vélez de Escalante, Silvestre
1995   *The Domínguez-Escalante Journal: Their Expedition through Colorado, Utah, Arizona, and New Mexico in 1776*, translated by Angélico Chávez, edited by Ted J. Warner. University of Utah Press, Salt Lake City.

Vierra, Bradley
1985   *Hunter-gatherer Settlement Systems: To Reoccupy or Not to Reoccupy, That is the Question.* Master's thesis, University of New Mexico, Albuquerque.

Vogler, Lawrence E.
1982   A Test of a Model of Prehistoric Subsistence and Settlement. In *Gallegos Mesa Settlement and Subsistence: A Set of Explanatory Models for Blocks VIII, IX, X, and XI, Navajo Indian Irrigation Project*, by Lawrence Vogler, Dennis Gilpin, and Joseph Anderson, pp. 339–405. Navajo Nation Papers in Anthropology No. 12, Vol, 1. Navajo Nation Cultural Resource Management Program, Window Rock, Arizona.

Wade, Edwin L., and Lea S. McChesney
1981   Historic Hopi Ceramics: The Thomas V. Keam Collection of the Peabody Museum of Archaeology and Ethnology, Harvard University. Peabody Museum Press, Cambridge, Massachusetts.

Ware, John A.
1981   Archaeological Investigations in the Durango District, Southwestern Colorado. *Contract Abstracts and CRM Archaeology* 2(2):20–28.

1986   The Prehistoric Sites. In *The Cultural Resources of Ridges Basin and Upper Wildcat Canyon*, edited by Joseph Winter, John Ware, and Phillip Arnold, pp. 147–194. Office of Contract Archeology, University of New Mexico, Albuquerque.

2002   What is a Kiva? The Social Organization of Early Pueblo Communities. In *Culture and Environment in the American Southwest: Papers in Honor of Robert C. Euler*, edited by David A. Phillips, Jr., and John A. Ware, pp. 79–88. SWCA Anthropological Research Papers No. 8. Phoenix.

Warren, A. H.
1986   Geological Resources. In *The Cultural Resources of Ridges Basin and Upper Wildcat Canyon*, edited by Joseph Winter, John Ware, and Phillip Arnold, pp. 25–44. Office of Contract Archeology, University of New Mexico, Albuquerque.

White, Richard
1991   *"It's Your Misfortune and None of My Own": A New History of the American West*. University of Oklahoma Press, Norman.

Wills, Wirt H.
1996   *Early Prehistoric Agriculture in the American Southwest*. School of American Research Press, Santa Fe.

Wilshusen, Richard
1989   Unstuffing the Estufa: Ritual Floor Features in Anasazi Pit Structures and Pueblo Kivas. In *The Architecture of Social Integration in Prehistoric Pueblos*, edited by William Lipe and Michelle Hegmon, pp. 89–111. Occasional Paper No. 1. Crow Canyon Archaeological Center, Cortez.

1999   Pueblo I (A.D. 750–900). In *Colorado Prehistory: A Context for the Southern Colorado River Basin,* edited by William D. Lipe, Mark D. Varien, and Richard H. Wilshusen, pp. 196–241. Colorado Council of Professional Archaeologists, Denver.

Wilson, C. Dean, and Eric Blinman
1993   *Upper San Juan Region Pottery Typology*. Archaeology Notes No. 80. Museum of New Mexico, Santa Fe.

1995a   Changing Specialization of White Ware Manufacture in the Northern San Juan Region. In *Ceramic Production in the American Southwest*, edited by Barbara J. Mills and Patricia L. Crown, pp. 63–87. University of Arizona Press, Tucson.

1995b   Ceramic Types of the Mesa Verde Region. In *Archaeological Pottery of Colorado: Ceramic Clues to the Prehistoric and Protohistoric Lives of the State's Native Peoples*, edited by Robert H. Brunswig, Jr., Bruce A. Bradley, and Susan M. Chandler, pp. 33–88. Occasional Papers No. 2. Colorado Council of Professional Archaeologists, Denver.

Windes, Thomas C.
1977   Typology and Technology of Anasazi Ceramics. In *Settlement and Subsistence along the Lower Chaco River*, edited by Charles A. Reher, pp. 279–370. University of New Mexico Press, Albuquerque.

Winter, Joseph C., John A. Ware, and Philip J. Arnold III (editors)
1986   *The Cultural Resources of Ridges Basin and Upper Wildcat Canyon*. Office of Contract Archeology, University of New Mexico, Albuquerque.

Wobst, H. Martin
1974   Boundary Conditions for Paleolithic Social Systems: A Simulation Approach. *American Antiquity* 39(2):147–178.

APPENDIX A

Animas–La Plata Archaeological Project
List of Proposed ALP Cultural Resources Volumes

Volume	Contents	Author(s)
I: Research Design	Project Research and Sampling Design	Dr. James Potter
II: Cultural Affiliation Study	Cultural Affiliation to Lands Comprised by ALP Project Area	Dr. Elizabeth Perry
III: Historic Archaeology	EuroAmerican Historic Archaeology and Protohistoric Archaeology	Dennis Gilpin and Tom Yoder
IV: Public Archaeology	Presentation of Project Results to the Public	Dr. James Potter
V–IX: Site Descriptions	Basic Site Descriptions	Various
X: Ceramics	All Ceramic Analyses	Dr. Jim Allison
XI: Lithics	Ground Stone, Flaked Stone, Projectile Points	Dr. Carl Phagan
XII: Bioarchaeology	Osteological and Burial Data	Dr. Elizabeth Perry
XIII: Environmental	Geomorphology, Botanical Analyses, Faunal Analyses, Catchment Analyses	Dr. Kirk Anderson, Dr. Karen Adams, Dr. James Potter
XIV: Administrative	Management and Quality Control Procedures and Policies, Database and GIS Background, Field and Laboratory Methods	Dr. James Potter, Tom Yoder, Danielle Desruisseaux
XV: Special Studies	Architecture, Ornaments, Bone/Wood Tools, Chronology, TCPs	Dr. James Potter, Tom Yoder, Dr. Carl Phagan, Dr. Elizabeth Perry
XVI: Synthetic	Response to Research Design, Project Overview	Dr. James Potter

APPENDIX B

Animas–La Plata Archaeological Project
Key Personnel for the ALP Project

Title	Name
Project Manager	Kevin Thompson
Principal Investigator and Director	Dr. James Potter
Field Director	Tom Yoder
Laboratory Director	Danielle Desruisseaux
Bioarchaeology Specialist	Dr. Elizabeth Perry
Paleobotany Specialist	Dr. Karen Adams
Lithics Specialist	Dr. Carl Phagan
Ceramics Specialist	Dr. James Allison
Geomorphologist	Dr. Kirk Anderson
Historic Archaeologist	Dennis Gilpin

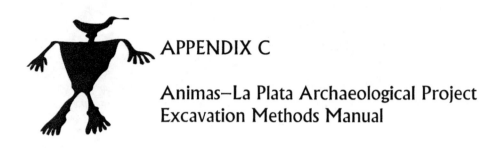

APPENDIX C

Animas–La Plata Archaeological Project Excavation Methods Manual

I. INTRODUCTION

This document is intended as a guide to the standard excavation methods and procedures used by SWCA Environmental Consultants for the Animas–La Plata Archaeological (ALP) Project. It is important to remember that archaeological field methods are designed to collect data relevant to both the specific questions posed by the archaeological research design and the nature of the archaeological resource. Thus, for any specific site or portion of a site, the methods used may differ slightly from those that are outlined in this document.

This manual addresses excavation techniques, field recordation (notes, maps, forms), field collection and treatment of artifacts and samples, and the protocol for turning artifacts, notes, and photographs over to the laboratory. Additional information and updates during the field season should be incorporated into this manual.

The purpose of data recovery through excavation is to provide information on past human and natural processes at sites that can be interpreted in an anthropological framework. Standard excavation techniques have emerged in Southwestern archaeology, and those presented below have been found to work well on sites in the ALP project area. However, everything considered "standard"—from unit size to level thickness, what is mapped, what is collected and how it is bagged, and so forth—can be modified depending on site-specific or project-specific questions.

Typically, the following minimum goals must be met by data recovery methods:

1. The natural processes and disturbances that have contributed to site formation must be identified and documented.

2. The cultural activities at the site must be identified and documented.

3. The spatial relationships (horizontal and vertical) among artifacts, natural features, cultural features, and disturbances must be identified and documented.

A constraining factor in all data recovery is that prior to excavation, the cultural and natural aspects of the site are mostly unknown. The methods used must enable control over relationships that may not be identified until all excavation has been completed. *Consequently, following a set of standard excavation techniques and documentation procedures is crucial.*

II. SITE MAPPING

Site mapping is comprehensively detailed in the *ALP Site Mapping Manual* and is only briefly discussed here. All sites in the project area will be mapped with a **Total Station**. The Total Station is a piece of equipment used to map sites using a laser-guided "gun" and a prism that reflects the laser beam back to the gun. The Total Station collects topographic data and establishes **horizontal** and **vertical control** across a site. The mapping crew will be responsible for the care of the equipment, downloading of data, and generation of maps from the data.

1. Grid – Horizontal Control

The **horizontal grid** will be established at the outset of work at any site. With the use of a Total Station the grid does not need to be physically marked across the entire site (e.g., grid nails every 2 m). Instead, horizontal grid points can be set as needed, allowing excavation areas to be tied together even if they are widely separated across a site.

The horizontal grid is based on the **primary site datum**. Grid *northings* increase to the north of the datum and decrease to the south of the datum (i.e., the farther north of the datum, the higher the northing number). Grid *eastings* increase to the east of the datum and decrease to the west of the datum (i.e., the farther east of the datum, the higher the easting number).

In general, the *southwest corner* of excavation units (1 × 1, 2 × 2, 10 × 10) will be used to designate its provenience. Grid centerpoints will be used to provenience features and feature portions.

2. Datums – Vertical Control

Vertical control is established from the primary site datum. All elevations across a site will be derived from this datum. Subdatums may be set adjacent to excavation areas to be more readily accessible. String lines are tied to the datum to allow measurements to be taken. Elevations are obtained by subtracting the number of centimeters below the string line and adding the number of centimeters above the string line.

For example, if a datum has an elevation of 100.0 m, and the bottom of an excavation unit is 56 cm below the string line, the elevation would be 99.44 m (100.00 m – 0.56 m = 99.44 m). If the top of a rubble mound is 45 cm above the string line, the elevation at the top of the mound would be 100.45 m (100.00 m + 0.45 m = 100.45 m).

III. THE PROVENIENCE DESIGNATION SYSTEM

The **Provenience Designation (PD) System** is the basis of the excavation methodology employed on the ALP project. An individual PD number represents the smallest distinct provenience (excavation level, feature stratum, surface collection unit, etc.) that can be *defined by the excavator*. Each provenience is a 3-dimensional unit of space that has horizontal and vertical parameters.

1. The PD Log

The PD Log (Figure C.1) records information specific to each PD number. It also functions to track artifacts and samples collected from each provenience. Each page of the PD Log contains space for multiple PD numbers.

A. Study Unit

The Study Unit is the largest level of investigation within a site. It is used to sub-divide large sites into smaller groups of related features. When no loci are identified, or the use of loci is not applicable, the default Study Unit will be *Whole Site*.

B. Horizontal and Vertical Codes

Every provenience will be given a horizontal and vertical code (see Figure C.2) that best defines what the excavator is attempting to describe.

Control Unit vs. Excavation Unit

A control unit is excavated in a known feature to provide a representative sample of fill. It is most often used in pit structures, where the majority of fill is not screened or excavated by stratum. An excavation unit is any arbitrary unit at a site, generally excavated either when a feature is not known to be present, or to define a feature such as a midden.

Trench Profile

This horizontal code is used when artifacts are collected from the sidewall of a mechanically excavated trench.

Prehistoric Use Surface

This designation refers both to floors within structures and to extramural surfaces that can be defined between features. In most cases, there will be only a single use surface (SURF-1). However, multiple floors are possible within structures, and they should be sequentially numbered (SURF-1, SURF-2, etc.).

Floor Contact vs. Surface Contact

Floors are generally within defined structures, whereas surfaces may occur in extramural areas. This vertical code is used for designating artifacts that were prehistorically deposited on a living/activity surface.

C. Artifact Codes

The artifacts and samples collected from each provenience are bagged by type, and the bags are numbered sequentially beginning with Bag 1. More than one bag can be used for each type of artifact—for example, there can be three bags of ceramics (Bags 1, 2, and 3). Codes (see Figure C.3) are used on the bags, and on data sheets, to identify artifact or material type.

PD #	SU	F #	Horiz	Vert	Strat	Level	PLs ✓	ARTIFACT BAGS		NONE ✓	COMMENTS	Closed ✓	Lab ✓
	☐ WS						☐	1-	6-	☐		☐	☐
	L___							2-	7-				
								3-	8-				
								4-	9-				
☐ cont.								5-	10-				

PD # - the number used to reference the provenience. The "cont." box beneath the number should be checked if the PD is continued on another page.
SU - the Study Unit within which the PD is located – Whole Site, or a particular Locus within the site.
F# - the Feature number within which the provenience occurs, if applicable.
Horiz - the Horizontal attribute of the PD number (see *Horizontal and Vertical Codes* below).
Vert - the Vertical attribute of the PD number (see *Horizontal and Vertical Codes* below).
Strat - the Stratum number associated with the PD (Roman numerals – I, II, III).
Level - the excavation level associated with the PD (Arabic numerals – 1, 2, 3).
PLs - checked if the PD number was assigned to a surface with Point Located artifacts on it.
Artifact Bags - lists the associated artifacts and samples, bagged by type (see *Artifact Codes*).
None - this box should be checked if no artifacts or samples were recovered from the PD.
Comments - allows for additional comments on the PD.
Closed - this box should be checked if no additional excavation data will be assigned to the PD #.
Lab - this box is checked by lab personnel when the PD is closed out and the artifact bags are turned into the lab.

Figure C.1. Example of PD log.

Horizontal Codes		Vertical Codes	
Backhoe Trench	BHT-#	Modern Surface	MS
Control Unit	CU-#	Overburden	OB
Excavation Unit	XU-#	Feature Fill	FF
Feature Portion	FP (FP W1/2, etc.)	Floor Fill (10 cm to floor)	FLF
Prehistoric Use Surface	SURF-#	Midden Fill	MF
Surface Collection Unit	SCU + PD #	Fill, not further specified	Fill NFS
Trench Profile	TP-#	Roof Fall	RF
Whole Feature	WF + Feature #	Wall Fall	WF
Whole Site	WS + PD #	Roof/Wall Fall	RWF
		Sterile	STL
		Floor Contact	FC
		Surface Contact	SC
		Other	OTH

Figure C.2. List of horizontal and vertical codes.

AMAG	Archaeomagnetic samples
BUR	All human bone, whether in intact burials or as isolated fragments
BOT	All vegetable, botanical, or plant remains
CER	Ceramics (includes all fired and unfired ceramics)
C14	Radiocarbon samples (charcoal)
DAUB	Daub and adobe (Note: daub with textile impressions should be classified as TEX)
DENDRO	Dendrochronological (tree-ring) samples
FAU	Faunal material (includes all worked and unworked animal bone, and animal burials) (Note: animal burials and worked bone must be bagged separately from all other unworked animal bone)
FLOT	Flotation samples
FLRS	Floor samples
FS	Flaked stone (includes lithic debitage, hammerstones, cores, angular debris [shatter])
GS	Ground stone (includes manos, metates, mauls, mortars, architectural stone, as well as worked ornaments, stone gaming pieces, and stone pipes)
PP	Projectile points
HIS	Historical artifacts (includes glass, metal, ceramics, and wood) (Note: historical artifacts should be bagged separately according to artifact class [glass, ceramic, metal, wood, etc.], with the artifact class noted in the Comments section of the bag label)
MIN	Includes worked and unworked minerals and unworked small stones and mineral specimens such as soapstone, talc, pigments, mica, quartz crystals, gypsum, schist, fossils, etc. May also include plaster and/or sediment samples taken for sourcing studies.
OBS	Obsidian (should always be bagged separately)
POL	Pollen samples
PHYTO	Phytolith samples and washes
SHL	Worked and unworked marine and freshwater shell (not eggshell, which is FAU)
TEX	Any type of woven or modified organic material (cordage, sandals, baskets, mats, etc.) or textile-impressed daub

Figure C.3. List of artifact and sample codes.

2. The PD Form

Every PD number on the PD Log requires an accompanying PD Form that fully describes the provenience. The PD Form allows for description of multiple PD numbers if they are of the same horizontal provenience (such as multiple fill strata from the south half of a hearth). Each form is composed of three basic parts, as illustrated in Figure C.4.

A. PD Codes – Fill Type Categories

Six PD Codes are used to *generally* classify the type of fill represented by the PD. The purpose of these codes is to clarify two things: (1) whether the fill is cultural and (2) how it got to where it is at the time of excavation.

Primary Cultural (PRI)

Refers to objects or fill deposited at their location of use or production. Debitage left at a flint knapper's work station, or the sherds from a dropped pot on the floor of a pit house, are examples. By convention, this concept has been extended to include feature deposits that are interpreted as associated with the use of the feature, such as ash and charcoal in a hearth. A further extension of this concept would include the accumulation of debris on a floor surface, surrounding a feature, or scattered across a use surface. Burned roof fall is considered a primary deposit if it is within a pit structure, but a secondary deposit if it is scattered around a midden. By convention, the 10 cm of fill above a floor surface (floor fill) is considered to be a primary deposit, unless a very strong argument can be made to the contrary.

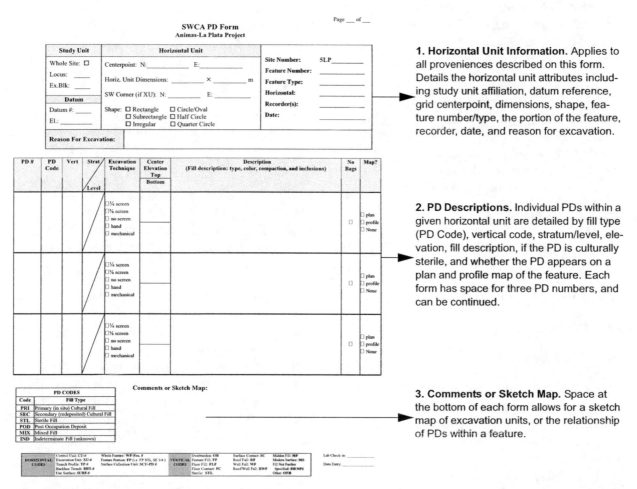

Figure C.4. Example of PD form.

Secondary Cultural (SEC)

Discarded or redeposited artifacts or fill. The implication is that the materials have been discarded away from their location of use or production. This category includes midden refuse.

Post-Occupation Deposit (POD)

Naturally deposited (e.g., by wind, water, gravity) stratum that may include some artifacts or culturally generated charcoal. Examples include the upper portions of pit house fill, charcoal-flecked blowsand that caps a midden deposit, or a deposit of water-laid sand that flowed into a vent shaft following the abandonment of a structure.

Sterile (STL)

Deposits that do not contain artifacts or *culturally generated* charcoal are considered sterile. The implication is that the deposit was not created or affected by cultural site formation processes.

Mixed (MIX)

A deposit containing a mix of two or more of the above types. This category is used most often when full-cut excavation of a feature portion cuts across more than one stratum. Activity such as looting, grazing, and erosion may also cause redeposition and mixing.

Indeterminate (IND)

The nature of deposition and the origin of artifacts or fill is unknown.

IV. EXCAVATION METHODOLOGY

1. Basic Concepts

A. Strata vs. Levels

A *stratum* is a layer of sediment that can be distinguished from overlying or underlying layers. The boundaries between strata can be defined by changes in texture, color, and/or inclusions. A stratum may be cultural or natural in origin.

A *level* is an arbitrary distinction made regardless of changes in texture, color, and/or inclusions. Levels are excavated within excavation units to maintain horizontal and vertical control over the provenience of artifacts. In most cases, excavation is conducted using arbitrary levels only when the stratigraphy is unknown.

Excavation may be done by strata, levels, or a combination of both. When excavating only by strata, level designations are not necessary but may be used if the deposits are complex. If levels are used within strata, they are numbered within each stratum beginning with Level 1. For example, if Levels 1–4 are excavated in Stratum II, the first level in Stratum III is Level 1, not Level 5. Likewise, if Stratum II has a Level 2, there must be a Stratum II, Level 1 designation. If excavation is in levels without identified strata, no stratum designations are used.

B. Forms vs. Logs

Data collected by excavation is recorded on two types of paperwork: forms and logs. *Forms* are descriptive, and specific to what is being excavated (feature, structure, excavation unit, etc.). *Logs* are used to keep track of forms, recording summary information from the forms. As discussed below, a variety of forms will be used on the ALP project, and each type of form has its own log.

C. Provenience Hierarchy

Any given site comprises smaller individual parts that make up the whole. These parts may be discussed individually (e.g., Feature) or as a group (e.g., Locus). As shown in Figure C.5, the parts may be organized in a hierarchy.

As shown in the figure, the largest (or highest) level of study is the *Site*. Each Site can be divided into smaller (or lower levels) of study, such as *Loci*. A Locus is made up of smaller units of study such as *Activity Areas*. An Activity Area consists of functionally or spatially related features, which may have *Subfeatures* within them. Both Features and Subfeatures contain smaller levels of study, such as strata or portions of strata. Activity Areas may also include *Excavation Units*, arbitrary units of study consisting of either portions of strata or arbitrary excavation levels that may cross-cut strata.

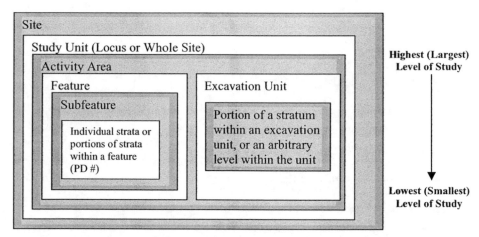

Figure C.5. Diagram of provenience hierarchy.

2. Excavation Methods

Excavation on the ALP project will generally start with the largest tool possible, then work down to smaller tools as need. The purpose of this approach is to investigate as much of the site as possible in the time allowed.

A. Mechanical Excavation

An archaeologist must be present constantly to monitor all mechanical excavation. Two mechanical excavation strategies are common: *trenching* and *surface scraping*.

Backhoe Trenching

A backhoe is used primarily to excavate exploratory trenches to locate cultural features, expose site stratigraphy, and test deep deposits. The trenches are generally excavated with a 24-inch-wide toothed bucket. For profiling, the walls of the trenches are faced by hand with trowel and shovel, removing gouges and smeared soils in order to observe the undisturbed sediments. Unproductive trenches are backfilled as soon as possible for logistical and safety reasons. The placement of the trenches is determined by the Crew Chief and Field Director, using both systematic and judgmental methods. Once features are exposed in a trench, they should be documented by profiling, describing, and photographing them. If a feature is not completely exposed within the trench, always expose the full vertical relief of the feature, even if the backhoe has to dig deeper in that area. Identifying the feature's location and presence is important, but accurate recording of a feature that has been impacted is even more so. Better to be thorough and clean than partially exposed and messy.

Backhoe Surface Scraping

To remove modern overburden sediments and post-abandonment deposits from over and within prehistoric features, a special 4-foot-wide bucket is used to strip the sediment away in systematic passes over an area. This wide bucket allows removal of the sediments in several consecutive, overlapping cuts only a few centimeters thick and leaves a smooth exposure that allows the monitoring archaeologist to examine the deposits and identify cultural features. Surface scraping is one of the quickest methods of assessing Pueblo I sites, as many of the deposits are shallow. Large areas of stripping are needed to adequately assess the surface remains of most sites in the ALP project area.

Artifacts that are recovered from the backdirt of mechanical excavation areas usually cannot be linked to a specific feature. These items should be provenienced by the PD number representing the backhoe trench or stripping area. Backhoe trenches are generally assigned a single PD number and logged on the Backhoe Trench Log. A backhoe-stripped area is considered a mechanically excavated Excavation Unit and should be logged on the Excavation Unit Log.

B. Hand Excavation – General Technique and Procedure

Standard Investigation Process

Although a variety of features will be encountered, the method of investigation is standard:

1. Define the feature horizontally and determine the uppermost limits. Often, this will also establish the *prehistoric ground surface (pgs)*.

2. Take a pre-excavation photograph of the feature.

3. Section (bisect, quarter, or trench) the feature in order to examine the fill sequence. If possible, excavation should be conducted by stratum. If stratigraphic excavation is not possible, then use arbitrary levels. All fill should be screened.

4. Photograph and draw the *stratigraphic profile*.

5. Excavate the remaining half stratigraphically, sampling each stratum as necessary. The Crew Chief should be consulted as to the sampling procedure. All other fill should be screened.

6. Take at least one final photograph of the feature.

7. Draw a *plan view map* of the feature at an appropriate scale. The standard scale for features is 1 inch = 20 cm, but if more detail is necessary, the scale can be changed.

8. Complete the Feature Form, PD Form(s), and Sample Form(s), and make sure that the PD Log is updated.

9. Have the Crew Chief review the paperwork and the completed excavation to ensure that all the information has been collected and properly recorded.

Human Remains

Excavation, analysis, and reporting of human remains are always conducted in a respectful and professional manner. If you suspect during the course of an excavation that you have encountered human bone, **stop** all excavation and notify the Crew Chief **immediately**. The methods for handling human remains are detailed in the *Human Remains Field Manual*.

3. Screening

All sediment will be screened through 1/4-inch mesh unless authorized by the Crew Chief. Smaller screen sizes (1/8 inch) may be used in certain situations, such as during excavation of burials.

A. Point Located Artifacts

Each artifact that is in contact with a defined surface (floor, bench, extramural use surface, roof fall, etc.) will be recorded on a *PL Log* (see Figure C.6) that is specific to the PD number assigned to the surface. A PL artifact may have multiple bag numbers if required (e.g., a large olla that will not fit into a single bag). The PL artifacts will also be logged into the Artifact Bag section of the *PD Log*, and the PL box should be checked.

Point-located artifacts can be collected from various contexts, depending on the position of the artifacts and where they occur. Figures C.7 and C.8 include two examples (scenarios) of how point-located artifacts may be collected from floor, secondary use, and roof-fall contexts.

PD No.	PL No.	Bag No.	Artifact Type	Grid Provenience	Elev.	Comments	Plotted? ✓
53	1	1	CER	N: 212.30 E: 330.20	100.01	Large olla, top half	☐
		2	CER	N: 212.30 E: 330.20	100.01	Large olla, bottom half (see Bag 1)	☐
	2	3	FS	N: 222.32 E: 332.20	100.01	Core	☐
	3	4	FS	N: 216.00 E: 330.85	100.01	Tool?	☐
	4	5	GS	N: 212.05 E: 329.20	100.01	Metate (in-field analysis)	☐

Figure C.6. Example of PL log.

PD #	SU	F #	Horiz	Vert	Strat	Level	PLs ✓	ARTIFACT BAGS				NONE ✓	COMMENTS	Closed ✓	Lab ✓
24	☐ WS L 2 ☐ cont.	11	SURF-1	RF	IV	I	☑	1- CER	2- FS	3- FS	4- GS	5-	6-	7-	8-	9-	10-	☐	Items associated with a re-use of the structure depression	☑	☐
61	☐ WS L 2 ☐ cont.	11	SURF-2	FC	--	--	☑	1- CER 2- CER 3- FS 4- GS 5- GS	6- CER 7- CER 8- CER 9- GS 10- GS			☐	Items on the latest floor surface	☑	☐
61	☐ WS L 2 ☐ cont.						☐	11- CER 12- CER 13- FS 14- GS 15- GS	16- CER 17- CER 18- CER 19- GS 20- GS			☐		☑	☐
98	☐ WS L 2 ☐ cont.	11	SURF-3	FC	--	--	☑	1- CER 2- CER 3- FS 4- GS 5- GS	6- CER 7- CER 8- CER 9- GS 10- GS			☐	Items on the earliest floor surface	☑	☐

Figure C.7. PL Scenario 1. A pit structure (Feature 11) with four fill strata is excavated in Locus 2. Strata I–III are post-occupation deposits, while Stratum IV is roof fall. A re-occupation of the structure depression is encountered as an irregular surface (designated SURF-1) on top of the roof fall. Two floor surfaces (SURF-2 and SURF-3) are encountered as two distinct plastered layers, each with features.

PD #	SU	F #	Horiz	Vert	Strat	Level	PLs ✓	ARTIFACT BAGS		NONE ✓	COMMENTS	Closed ✓	Lab ✓
17	□ WS L⊥	2	WF-2	RF	II	1	☑	1- CER 2- FS 3- FS 4- GS 5- CER	6- CER 7- FS 8- OBS 9- PP 10- FS	□	Items likely stored in the roof of the structure	☑	□
□ cont.													
17	□ WS L⊥						□	11- CER 12- CER 13- FS 14- GS 15- GS	16- CER 17- CER 18- CER 19- GS 20- GS	□		☑	□
□ cont.													
98	□ WS L⊥	2.01	WF-2.01	SC	--	--	☑	1- CER 2- CER 3- FS 4- GS 5- GS	6- CER 7- CER 8- 9- 10-	□	Items on the bench surface	☑	□
□ cont.													
134	□ WS L⊥	2	SURF-1	FC	--	--	☑	1- CER 2- CER 3- FS 4- GS 5- GS	6- CER 7- CER 8- PP 9- PP 10-	□	Items on the floor surface	☑	□
□ cont.													

Figure C.8. PL Scenario 2. A pit strucgture (Feature 2) with two fill strata is excavated in Locus 1. Stratum I is sterile post-occupation fill, and Stratum II is roof fall. Artifacts are found on top of and within the roof fall (Stratum II), and it is decided that they represent artifacts stored in the roof. They are point located, as are items on the bench (Feature 2.01) and floor surface.

Note: Each PD number for both Scenario 1 and Scenario 2 would have a PL Log to document the artifact locations.

B. Artifact Recovery

Artifacts are generally grouped together and bagged by class (e.g., flaked stone, bone, ceramics, etc.). The following artifacts should be bagged separately:

- Flaked stone tools, including projectile points

- Any obsidian artifacts—each obsidian tool should get a separate bag, and obsidian debitage should be bagged separately from any other debitage

- Ground stone artifacts

- Worked bone, such as awls

- Beads and decorative objects (figurines, carved shell, etc.)

- Whole, or nearly complete, glass or ceramic vessels (prehistoric or historical)

- Any unique or fragile artifacts

In addition, a ground stone artifact may be a source of pollen in the form of a *pollen wash*. Thus, it is important to handle these artifacts properly in the field. *All* ground stone artifacts recovered in situ should be protected for potential pollen washing. The only exception is ground stone recovered from the modern surface of a site. After exposure of the artifact, leave as much of the dirt matrix as possible in or on the artifact to protect the use surface. Then cover the surface and the artifact as quickly as possible, preferably with aluminum foil or a sealed plastic bag.

C. Sample Collection

The primary method for recording data on samples is the *General Sample Form*. Brief descriptions of the more common types of samples collected during excavations and the methods to be used for each are provided here.

Radiocarbon (¹⁴C) sampling is one of the most common forms of chronometric sampling used in any excavation. Annual plant remains such as corncobs or kernels, matting or textiles, juniper berries, piñon cones or nuts, or similar materials provide the best samples. Burned fuel wood from thermal fea-

tures is most commonly encountered. In the case of wood charcoal, small twigs and branches are preferable to larger interior wood fragments. A sample size of 30 g (about the size of a golf ball) is ideal for conventional radiocarbon dating. Smaller sample sizes (less than one gram) are needed for the accelerator mass spectrometry (AMS) method of dating. Always avoid contact between the charcoal sample and any foreign material, such as lotion, bug spray, food, or cigarette ashes. Always use a trowel or other steel tool to collect the samples, and store them in foil packets.

Dendrochronological samples provide the best chronometric data and are preferable to ¹⁴C samples when datable material is available. Dendrochronological dating is based on matching the growth rings of wood fragments to a master key that has been well dated. As such, the greater the number of rings in a sample, the more accurately it can be matched to the key, and the more accurate the date. However, small fragments of wood with as few as 10 rings may yield a date, and it should be stressed that samples do not need to be limited to large intact beams. Wood fragments with bark are ideal samples, as the last year that the tree was alive is recorded by the outermost ring. Information yielded by dendrochronological samples includes the season in which structures were built, remodeling events and length of occupation, salvaging of other structures, and selection of wood species by the prehistoric occupants.

Flotation samples are collected to recover macrobotanical remains of economic plant species, such as corncobs or kernels, beans, squash seeds or rind fragments, and wild plant seeds, berries, and other fragments. Flotation samples taken from features and subfeatures should consist of 2 liters of sediment, ideally recovered from a single unmixed context. Samples smaller than 2 liters should also be retained if the feature or subfeature is very small. Flotation samples should be placed in clean, doubled paper bags and the top folded over and taped down with masking tape for transportation to the laboratory. Flotation samples reflect the function of the feature that is being sampled, such as storage or processing. Contexts that have been sealed by catastrophic burning or that retain primary fill are the most desirable sampling contexts.

If significant deposits of *macrobotanical* materials are encountered, they should be separated from regular flotation samples. Items such as burned matting, textiles, and wooden artifacts and stored economic materials such as corn should be carefully packaged and submitted to the laboratory as BOT (botanical) samples. Radiocarbon samples may also be extracted from these materials if the quantity is sufficient. If excess macrobotanical remains are present even after BOT and ^{14}C samples have been recovered, the remainder may be submitted as an additional flotation sample and noted on the sample bag.

Pollen samples are used to identify prehistoric economic plant use, determine the surrounding prehistoric vegetation, reveal specific uses of features, and evaluate environmental changes or shifts in plant use through time. Samples should consist of at least 4–6 tablespoons of sediment collected with a clean trowel and placed in a self-sealing bag.

Pollen samples will be collected from a variety of contexts. Sealed contexts (e.g., beneath artifacts on a floor, the primary fill of a pit), should be rigorously sampled. Overlying post-occupation fill should also be sampled to provide a comparison between natural pollen and economic pollen. To this end, the prehistoric ground surface and modern ground surface at each site will also be sampled. Composite sampling of floor surfaces will be conducted in every structure, and sub-floor excavation should not commence until this procedure has been completed.

In-situ artifacts (metates, mealing bin slabs, manos) should be covered with foil immediately upon removal for later pollen washing. When artifacts containing dirt (pipes, vessels, metate troughs, etc.) are encountered, the dirt should *not* be removed in the field.

D. Filling Out Artifact Bags

The artifact bag is the *only way* to tie an artifact to its provenience in the ground. It is therefore critical that the information on the bag be completed properly in the field. Each artifact bag is stamped or printed with lines for all the information that is essential for tracking that artifact/those artifacts during the excavation. The bag stamp includes the following information:

1. Site Number

2. PD Number

3. Bag Number

4. Feature Number (if applicable)

5. Date

6. Excavator Initials

7. Comments (if necessary)

Photodocumentation

Photography is a crucial aspect of site recording. After excavation of a site is completed, much of what was excavated is gone, and the photographs are the only detailed visual record of the site. Take more photographs than necessary, not fewer.

Minimally, the following photographs should be taken:

1. *Site overviews* – provide shots of the site from various angles that characterize the site setting and environment prior to and during excavation.

2. *Features* – take a photograph of the plan view, the profile, and the feature after excavation. Take more photographs during excavation to show details of any features that are present.

3. *Artifacts* – take photographs of significant artifacts and artifact concentrations found in situ.

4. *Feature/surface/activity area shots* – remember to take overviews of significant broad exposures such as activity surfaces, feature groups, structure groups, etc.

E. Mapping Standards

Various plan views, cross sections, and profiles are created during data recovery investigations. *A feature is not fully documented until a plan view map and stratigraphic profile are completed.* Whenever possible, put the plan map and profile on the same page.

Plan View Map

A *plan view* is essentially a map showing the horizontal extent of excavated areas and cultural phenomena. These maps may vary greatly in scale and focus and may show the entire site or a single feature. Structure plan views focus on the location of subfeatures and floor contact artifacts. It may also be helpful to maintain multiple maps of some features, with one set of maps showing the archaeological aspects of the feature and another set showing the location and boundaries of excavated units.

All plan view maps should include the following:

1. scale and north arrow

2. at least two grid points

3. a standardized key

4. the plane of bisection or profile line (indicated as A–A')

5. site number, feature number, date, name of recorder

Stratigraphic Profile

Stratigraphic profiles record the extent and thickness of various deposits that are exposed on a vertical face, such as in the wall of a trench or excavation unit. Profiles graphically record the depositional sequence in a feature. They should be drawn at the same scale as the plan view map. Detailed descriptions of each fill stratum are recorded on the PD Form.

All stratigraphic profiles should include the following:

1. scale

2. bisection points (A–A') that correspond to the plan view map

3. brief descriptions of the strata below the profile; detailed descriptions are recorded on the PD Form

4. strata labeled with Roman numerals (I, II, III, etc.) and PD numbers

5. site number, feature number, date, name of recorder

Architectural *Cross Section*

Architectural cross sections differ from stratigraphic profiles in that they outline the vertical relationships of the physical features in a structure, such as the height of the walls and the depth of the hearth. Architectural cross sections should be drawn at the same scale as the plan view map.

All architectural cross sections should include the following:

1. scale

2. bisection points (A–A') that correspond to the plan view map

3. labeled subfeatures

4. modern ground surface (mgs) or prehistoric ground surface (pgs)

5. site number, feature number, date, project number, name of recorder (if on a separate page from the plan view)

What is North?

There are three meanings of north in archaeology, and no mention of north is complete without a qualifier indicating which meaning is being referenced.

Magnetic North. The direction of the magnetic north pole, which moves over time and toward which a compass needle will point. *Magnetic north is not used on the ALP project.*

True North. The direction to the axis around which the earth rotates, as opposed to the direction of the magnetic pole. A compass reading of north is True North when the declination is correctly set (14° west in Durango) to compensate for this difference.

Grid North. Grid north is a creation of the archaeologist and refers to the direction designated as north on the grid system. In general, Grid North will be the same as True North.

V. FORMS

Forms are one of the most important **parts** of recording data in the field. Figure C.9 presents a **list** of forms that will be used during the ALP project. **Two** general rules apply to the use of forms. First, fill **out all** parts of any given form or make a note that no information is applicable to that section (N/A). Second, be as descriptive as possible and use this information to make some interpretations. A more thorough interpretation of the archaeology will be done when all of the analysis has been completed and a full set of data is available.

Form	Function
Activity Area Summary Form	Synthesizes data, describes the relationship of features to one another, and relates them to associated artifacts. In general, every feature will have its own set of forms, and the Activity Area Summary Form will be used as a means of collating the information.
Auger Form	Records data for every auger probe conducted when testing for subsurface features.
Backhoe Trench Log	Summarizes backhoe exploration trenches by number, PD number, grid location, depth, size, related features, and date.
Continuation Form	Appended to any form when more space for explanation is required.
Digital Photo Log	Records relevant data for each photograph, including JPEG number, subject of photo, direction of photo, and date that the photo was taken.
Feature Form	Records individual features and is accompanied by a plan view map and profile. Records feature morphology, provenience, method of construction, fill description, and function.
Feature Summary Log	Records all features and subfeatures at a site. Not all subfeatures will have a Feature Form, and that data will be included on this form.
Field Burial Form	Records data on human remains for each burial.
General Sample Form	Accompanies every sample, summarizes the context, and rates the data potential.
Isolated Human Remains Log	Expedient method for documenting isolated human bones.
PD Form	Records data for individual PD numbers. *This form is filled out for every PD.* The PD Form functions as the primary method of recording data from Excavation Units as well as from Features.
Journal Form	Used by the Crew Chief to record daily notes on the site.
PD Log	Tracks every PD number assigned at a site. Every provenience is summarized by Study Unit, Horizontal Unit, Vertical Unit, and artifacts recovered. In addition, the PD Log records whether a particular provenience has been closed out (completed).
PL Log	Records data on individual point-located artifacts on a floor or surface. Data includes PD number, artifact bag number, artifact type, horizontal (grid) provenience, and vertical (elevation) provenience. Each surface, whether it is in a structure or outside of a structure, will have its own PL log.
Pit Structure Form	Primary method of synthesizing data on pit structures. Discusses attributes of subfeatures in relation to architecture, abandonment process, function, artifact assemblage, and morphology.
Summary of Unexcavated Burials	General site-level summary of unexcavated burials describing why they were not excavated, their locations, and the probability of finding additional burials at the site.
Unexcavated Burial Log	Tracks each unexcavated burial at a site, including when it was discovered, the feature numbers assigned, type of remains, condition, location, and level of documentation.
XU Log	Tracks and describes each assigned Excavation Unit (XU), including number, location, and dimensions.

Figure C.9. Excavation record forms and their functions.

VI. FEATURES

Features are the products of prehistoric **cultural** activity at a site. They should be thought of in **two** broad categories: *architectural* and *non-architectural*. Both architectural and non-architectural **features** may have *subfeatures* within them.

1. Architectural Feature

An architectural feature is a cultural unit of space with definable **boundaries** that may or may not have been walled, **but** has evidence of having been roofed. Evidence of a discrete floor or use-compacted surface is generally **required** for interpretation as an architectural remnant **when** no walls or remains of a roof support system are evident.

2. Non-Architectural Feature

A non-architectural feature is a cultural unit of space that is not necessarily roofed or bounded by walls but has definable boundaries. These features should exhibit some kind of evidence to suggest that they were constructed rather than natural in origin. Non-architectural features may be either sitting on top of the prehistoric surface (e.g., Thermal Refuse Pile, Midden) or dug into the surface (e.g., Ash Pit, Hearth).

3. Subfeature

A subfeature may be *within* or *part of* either an architectural or a non-architectural feature. A subfeature is defined as: (a) any feature that was part of, or within, an architectural feature; (b) a feature built within a non-architectural feature, such as a re-use of a roasting pit; or (c) an element associated with the function of a non-architectural feature, such as a pile of burned refuse rock adjacent to a roasting pit. Subfeatures are designated by a numerical suffix (.##) to the feature number (e.g., a hearth in Feature 3 may be designated F3.01). Table C.1 lists and defines the feature types that will be used during the ALP project.

Table C.1. Feature Types for the Animas–La Plata

Feature Type	Definition
Animal Burial	The whole or partial articulated skeleton of any non-human animal, excluding post-occupation intrusives such as rodents. An animal burial does not have to be in a pit or necessarily associated with another feature.
Ash Pit	Small features, usually within structures, that were used to contain ashes. Ash pits are usually found in association with a hearth. These types of features may have functioned as warming basins.
Bell Shaped Pit	As the name implies, these pits are dug into the ground and flare out toward their bases. These features can be more than 2 m deep and are often difficult to detect because the upper portion has filled with clean sediment. Some may have slabs in the upper fill from a collapsed superstructure. Bell shaped pits are associated with storage, and several are often found together.
Bench	A raised area around the perimeter of a pit structure in which stringer posts are set. The bench is an architectural element that was also used to store objects.
Bin	Bins are often found in the back corners of Pueblo I pit structures, although they have also been found in the front corners adjacent to wing walls. They are usually built of some combination of adobe, posts, and slabs. Bins often stand the same height as the bench, and it is not uncommon for them to be as large as 1 m in diameter. They are associated with food storage.
Borrow Pit	Pit or hollow created prehistorically by the removal of sediment for use elsewhere, generally for construction.
Check Dam	A collection of rocks, usually cobble sized, placed in a drainage to either collect sediment or divert water.
Cobble Apron/ Ring	Generally found downslope of pit structures and are crescent-shaped. Cobble rings surround pit structures and any associated surface rooms. Both are made of unshaped gravels, cobbles, and light refuse, with little or no depth. Both cobble aprons and rings are between 0.5 and 2.0 m in width. Cobble rings may be associated with stockades.
Deflector	Deflectors are found in pit structures, and rarely in surface structures. They are built of adobe, posts and adobe, or simply an upright slab anchored into the floor. Deflectors are found between the hearth and the ventilator opening. In some cases, an ash pit is found between the hearth and the deflector.
Deflector Slot	A longitudinal depression in the floor of a structure where a deflector slab was placed.
Fire Pit	An informally constructed pit that usually shows signs of thermal use, such as oxidation. Fire pits are generally unlined and of earthen construction.
Glyph	A character or figure that is carved, incised, or painted on a non-portable object, for example, a pecked figure on a boulder adjacent to a surface room, or an incised design in the plaster of a pit structure wall.
Hearth	A formally constructed pit that usually shows signs of thermal use, such as oxidation. Stone or adobe plaster are usually incorporated into its construction.
Inhumation	The deliberate deposit of a human body, whether it is buried in a pit or laid on the floor of an abandoned structure. Most PI period inhumations involve burial in a pit with grave goods.
Isolated Human Remain	Human remains that are incomplete or have evidently been disturbed. This feature type is for eroded human remains and those that have been disturbed by looting.
Kiln	Features built to contain the process of firing pottery. PI period kilns are rectangular to oval slab-lined pits, which when found archaeologically contain the residue of pottery firing, including a thin lens of charcoal above the slabs and possibly sherd "wasters", under-fired or over-fired sherds.

Table C.1. Feature Types for the Animas–La Plata Project, continued

	Definition
Ladder Sockets	Small holes in the floors of pit structures that are interpreted as anchoring the ladder that was used to enter the subterranean chamber. They are usually located around the deflector, as the entry hole was generally above the hearth.
Linear Ridge	A low ridge of adobe or a pole covered with adobe on the floor of a pit structure. The ridge outlines areas and spatial divisions within the structure as defined by the inhabitants.
Mealing Bin	Although usually found within structures, mealing bins also occur in extramural contexts. They are usually rectangular with upright slab or adobe walls and are often found with the metate in place. They are usually found in post-PI contexts. PI sites generally do not have formal mealing bins. The empty shallow pits found in many pit structures may have served a similar function.
Midden	Formal trash area of a site, usually south or east of a pit structure. Most PI sites in the Durango area have thin sheet middens with little or no depth. Staining may or may not be present.
Niche	Niches are small recesses dug into the walls of pit structures. They are much smaller than wall cists, and are associated with storage or caching of small items.
Non-cultural Feature	Feature type assigned post-excavation. The Feature Summary Table will have a more detailed description of the reason for the non-cultural designation.
Other	Used when no other feature type fits the feature designation. The feature is described in the Feature Summary Table.
Oxidized Spot	An area of localized fire-reddening and/or charring on a surface, may be accompanied by overlying fill. This type of feature represents an expedient fire built on the surface.
Paho Marks	Paho marks, or prayer stick impressions, differ from sipapus in size and depth, usually being 1–2 cm in diameter and 2–5 cm deep. Like sipapus, they are often filled in with clean sand and are found along the main axes of pit structures.
Passage Way	Found in pit rooms or pit structures that have a ramped or tunnel entry. Passage ways also connect antechambers to the main chamber of pit structures (pre–AD 750).
Pit (NFS)	Category used only when a pit has no evidence of use, such as oxidation, and the exact function cannot be determined.
Pit Room	Semisubterranean room that may be slab lined. Pit rooms may be isolated or occur in non-contiguous arcs. Pit rooms are more than 30 cm in depth below the prehistoric surface.
Pit Structure	Subterranean structures that include both primary domestic structures and special use/integrative structures (protokivas). Pit structures in the Durango area are between 3.5 and 8 m in diameter and up to 2.5 m deep. Most have an encircling bench, 4–6 main support posts, at least one sipapu, and wing walls, and are oriented southeast. Vent openings may be bifurcated (two openings).
Pit w/ Burning	A pit that exhibits some evidence of thermal activity, such as light oxidation, but no other evidence to infer use.
Plaza	Plazas are extramural features that functioned as formalized outdoor activity areas within the bounds of a household compound. This designation should not be used unless there is strong evidence of a formal or prepared surface within a household compound.
Post Hole	As the name implies, a hole that once held a post or contains a post remnant. Post holes are usually cylindrical and vary in both depth and diameter.
Ramada	An unwalled shade structure, usually defined by post holes and a use compacted surface that may or may not have features and artifacts present.
Roasting Pit	These features are usually apparent on the surface as darkly stained soil with burned rock. The dark fill suggests a reducing or oxygen-starved context, where the fuel was not burned to ash. Oxidation may occur around the rim of these features but is not usually found within them. Many are slab lined or incorporate rocks to retain and radiate heat for roasting. Roasting pits were used to process both vegetal and faunal material. These features may be up to 2 m deep and 1 m in diameter.
Rock Alignment	An alignment of at least three rocks with some evidence of cultural origin. Rock alignments may also represent structure remnants.
Rock Cluster	Groups of unshaped rock that are somewhat horizontally discrete and appear to be cultural in origin, but do not have a readily apparent function. This type of feature may also represent poorly preserved portions of a structure.
Rock Pile	Discrete groups of unburned, unshaped rock that appear to be cultural in origin but do not have a readily apparent function.

Table C.1. Feature Types for the Animas–La Plata Project, continued

	Definition
Sipapu	A small, usually cylindrical pit defined by its location along the primary axis of a pit structure. In general, a sipapu will be in line with the hearth, ash pit, deflector, and vent shaft. It may be immediately adjacent to the hearth, or farther back, closer to the back wall of the structure. Very often sipapus have been filled in with clean sand and capped. It is not uncommon for PI sipapus to be paired or occur in multiples as a "sipapu complex". Paho marks may also be found in association with sipapus. Sipapu fill should be collected as a pollen sample, as it will often contain culturally modified levels of pollen.
Slab Lined Pit	A circular or square pit dug into the earth and lined with slabs. A basal slab may or may not be present. If there is no evidence of thermal activity, it is likely associated with storage. Pits with darkly stained fill likely functioned as roasting features.
Stockade	An enclosure that surrounds a habitation. Stockades were constructed of upright posts and vary in robustness. Some appear to have been built of posts up to 30 cm in diameter, while others appear to have been built of brush. The presence of burned adobe suggests that some may have also been mudded. They are generally visible as post hole alignments or linear smears of charcoal and adobe.
Storage Pit	A non-thermal feature that may or may not have a formal lining, but exhibits some evidence of having been used primarily for storage. The storage function is implied by the absence of thermal alteration, the presence of stored goods, or the location of the feature within a structure or at the site. Unless there is a strong argument or line of reasoning for a pit to be interpreted as a storage feature, it should be designated Pit NFS.
Stringer Posts	Inward-leaning timbers that supported earthen coverings of mud and brush that formed the walls of structures.
Surface Room	As the name implies, these features generally originate at the prehistoric ground surface level, or slightly below the surface. Most had walls built of posts covered with adobe that were footed on unshaped cobbles or sandstone slabs. Floors were often unprepared, although some were floored with slabs or had a floor of adobe and wood. Surface rooms may be isolated or contiguous.
Thermal Refuse Pile	Discrete concentrations of refuse that originate on either a floor surface or a use surface. Most often found immediately adjacent to a thermal feature, and represents one or multiple clean-outs of the feature. These types of features can consist of ash, burned rock, charcoal, burned bone, and/or artifacts.
Thermal Refuse Pit	A pit containing a discrete concentration of refuse that originates on either a floor surface or a use surface. Most often found immediately adjacent to a thermal feature, and represents one or multiple clean-outs of the feature. These types of features can contain ash, burned rock, charcoal, burned bone, and/or artifacts.
Ventilator Shaft	A vertical tunnel that connects to a horizontal vent tunnel to form the ventilator system of a pit structure. Vent shafts are generally 1 m in diameter and originate at the prehistoric ground surface.
Ventilator System	Ventilator systems are components of pit structures. They are comprised of two parts: (1) a vertical shaft 0.5 to 1.5 m in diameter approximately 1.5 m south/southeast of the structure and (2) a horizontal tunnel leading from the structure chamber to the base of the vertical shaft. Many pit structures in the Durango area have a bifurcated ventilator system, that is, the horizontal tunnel has two openings into the structure. Many times these openings are coped with adobe. When the Ventilator Shaft and Ventilator Tunnel are excavated together, it may make more sense to discuss them together as the Ventilator System rather than as individual components.
Ventilator Entry	A pit structure subfeature that functions as both a ventilator and an entry into the structure. This feature type includes entries that may have been remodeled into vents during the use of the structure.
Ventilator Tunnel	The horizontal component of a ventilator system. These tunnels connect with vent shafts to form an L-shaped conduit that opens into a structure at or close to floor level. Ventilator tunnel openings may be bifurcated (have two holes) and coped.
Wall Cist	A pit dug into the wall of a pit structure. Cists are usually found at the lower wall/floor junction and may go back more than 1 m into the wall. Many are plastered or incorporate slabs in their construction. Wall cists are associated with storage.
Wing Wall	A feature that divided space within a pit structure. They may be constructed of posts and adobe, upright slabs, or a combination of posts, adobe, and rock. The area in front of the wing wall (between the front structure wall and the wing wall) was often used for storage of tools and milling equipment. It is common for wing walls to be connected to the deflector, forming a low partition across the front of the structure. Apertures are often found in wing walls, functioning to allow air or objects to pass through.
Wing Wall Aperture	An opening in a wing wall that allowed objects or air to pass through, but was not large enough for a person to crawl through. Apertures are less than 50 cm in diameter, and may be found at any point along a wing wall.